MOVE FORWARD CONFIDENTLY

Move Forward
Confidently

A WOMAN'S GUIDE TO NAVIGATING
THE HIGH-NET-WORTH DIVORCE

Patrick J. Kilbane J.D., CDFA®
and Caitlin Frederick, CFA, CPA

LIONCREST
PUBLISHING

MOVE FORWARD CONFIDENTLY

A Woman's Guide to Navigating the High-Net-Worth Divorce

ISBN   978-1-5445-0490-2 *Paperback*

978-1-5445-0489-6 *Ebook*

The stories used in this book are based on real clients; however, names, circumstances, and identifying details have been changed to protect and respect their privacy. These accounts may not precisely mirror your own life and situation, but it is our hope that by sharing them, you will find parallels and relevant, useful information. A glossary of key words (italicized upon first reference) can be found at the end of the book in the appendix.

Contents

Introduction

Because you opened this book, you're likely considering divorce (or know somebody who is) or are in the thick of it, and many of the questions on your mind are financial: How will I pay for college for my children? Will my lifestyle be dramatically reduced? What about alimony and child support? Am I going to be left with nothing?

Our goal is to provide you with a clear, comprehensive understanding of the divorce process. Think about the first thing you see when you enter an amusement park. A kiosk usually stands at the entrance with a map and a corresponding list showing where each ride is located. A big dot on the map displays your current position in relation to everything else. The dot is marked with the words "YOU ARE HERE." Just like that kiosk map, we will show you where you currently are and how to get to the next place you need (and want) to go, as well as how to prevent mistakes—particularly financial ones.

We will break down the journey for you, step by step. With this guidebook, our intention is to help you create a plan for the future and gain the confidence and knowledge you need to navigate it.

We bring over twenty years of experience and expertise in family law and wealth management to the writing of this book. Pat worked as one of Northeast Florida's most respected family law attorneys for years and is also a Certified Divorce Financial Analyst™ (CDFA®) and Wealth Manager. Caitlin is a Certified Financial Analyst® (CFA®) and a Certified Public Accountant (CPA). She leads the financial planning process for our clients. Our experiences make us uniquely qualified to fill a gap—helping women navigate their divorces and providing the financial planning needed to help them create a rock-solid future. We're extremely passionate about our work because we know the quality of our clients' lives correlates to their financial health. Further, because of our experience, we understand how stressful and intimidating a divorce can be. We want to alleviate as much uncertainty as possible.

Please be aware that our discussion of the legal process throughout the book pertains to Florida law and procedure. Although procedures and laws differ from state to state, there are many similarities to the discussion of divorce in general terms. Also, even though Pat is a lawyer, he is not providing any legal advice to our clients. His expertise allows him to help our clients understand the divorce process and help their lawyers spot issues.

DIVORCE IS NOT UNCOMMON

It is important to know you're not alone, neither the first person to go through a divorce nor the last. Approximately one-third of our clients, as well as prospective ones, are divorced. Recent government statistics show approximately 40 to 50 percent of first marriages end in divorce. This number increases for second and third marriages.

Many women going through a divorce feel betrayed and hurt by the person they trusted most in the world. Others are the primary income earners or business owners who want to protect what they've built. Either way, they often feel trapped and want to exit the marriage as quickly as possible. Fears abound, including one of not being able to support themselves at anything close to the standard of living that they enjoyed during their marriage. (Millions of women have this worry; a 2013 study reported in *Forbes* magazine found that over 25 percent of the women polled with household incomes of $200,000 per year or more said they feared losing their money and ending up homeless.[1])

One of the biggest steps you can take at this moment is to view what lies ahead as a business decision, not an emotional one. By calling on your inner strength and taking control, you'll lay the groundwork for a successful outcome. It is not easy for any of us to admit we don't know something, especially when the stakes are high. We congratulate you on taking the steps necessary to successfully navigate your divorce and to educate yourself on the process. By doing so, you are on the right track to managing your future.

DISCOVERING YOURSELF IN DIVORCE

It is paramount for your lawyer—and all other professionals with whom you will be working during your case—to understand who you are, not only from a financial standpoint but from a personal one as well. We call gaining a deep understanding of a person the "Life Map" process.

The Life Map begins with an extensive interview. We ask detailed questions about your goals, values, interests, advisors, assets, and relationships. You explain your

---

1   Allianz, "The Allianz Women, Money, and Power Study: Empowered and Underserved," 2013, https://www.allianzlife.com/-/media/files/allianz/documents/ent_1462_n. pdf?la=en&hash=DB76F6EE3B711B77523AABC237F9B37F6E8F2F21.

values as well as what—and who—is important to you. The Life Map helps us gain a deep perspective into what motivates you and what you would like your new life to look like. In many cases, it assists clients in learning more about themselves and helps in reevaluating priorities. The product of this extensive interview is your personalized Life Map, a one-page infographic to which every member of our wealth management team has access. It allows our team to get to know our clients at great depth. Further, the Life Map can be used in meetings with your lawyer and other members of your team to ensure everyone is on the same page regarding your goals and priorities. (For an expanded discussion of the Life Map, see Chapter 8; a graphic illustrating the process can be found in the appendix.)

In the beginning of the divorce process, and when creating a Life Map, many women cannot identify their goals and desires, and perhaps, at this point, you can't either. This is normal. Insecurity, confusion, even bewilderment are by-products of divorce in its initial stages, as is the feeling of not being able to trust anyone. Occasionally, some women develop the false belief that they do not deserve a portion of the marriage's finances because they didn't "earn" it.

One of the most important things to do from the start is to surround yourself with professionals who will competently guide you through the numerous financial and business decisions ahead. Now is the time to make the most informed and educated decisions possible. In a divorce, once the assets are divided and a deal struck, it is generally irreversible. There is no turning back. Too many women going through a divorce assume they can "start over"—perhaps go back to school and train for a new career. They don't ask or pursue enough financial resources to do so. Other women succumb to intimidation tactics or agree to not use attorneys—to their detriment. This is why it is extremely important to put together a competent team of professionals who will help ensure the most successful outcome.

METAMORPHOSIS

When we think of a metamorphosis or a drastic change, we frequently visualize a caterpillar morphing into a beautiful butterfly. However, the truth is that before the caterpillar can take flight, it goes through a process of substantial growth and change inside the protection of the chrysalis.

In the same way, before your new life can begin, key components of the old one must be dismantled, carefully and deliberately. In this book, we will describe each stage of the divorce process—from the first moment to the *final judgment* and beyond. Further, we will outline the financial aspects of divorce and offer best practices for identifying a strong professional team of advisors. Even before the divorce is over, you should have a clear idea of the kind of lifestyle you'll be able to live. Countless women go through divorce and come out on the other side with happier, more fulfilling lives. Transformation happens. The key formula is solid guidance, expertise, and a dose of optimism. This book provides you with all three.

CHAPTER ONE

You've Got This

In marriage, women frequently take a back seat when it comes to managing their finances, despite their level of education and capabilities. Many of our clients have been married to alpha males who have controlled and managed everything, from retirement accounts to taxes to investment property. The advisors your husband has relied on may be people you have known and liked for years, such as your CPA, attorney, or wealth manager. You may have even socialized with them regularly. Unfortunately, they may not always be the people to turn to for help when it comes to your divorce.

For example, your CPA may have a conflict of interest if he or she also represents your husband's business. You may be more comfortable establishing a new relationship with a CPA disassociated from your husband and his business. In fact, it is our strong recommendation for you to establish your own team of advisors. Think of your divorce as being similar to longtime partners in a business deciding to go their separate ways. In that scenario, business partners each have separate attorneys, business appraisers, and other advisors to consider each partner's interests and help negotiate and execute the deal. If you are an alpha female and have been the primary breadwinner in your relationship, it is likely that you may choose to stay with your current team of advisors. This will generally be the case if you are the one who has proactively handled those relationships in the past.

In Chapter 2, we will discuss in detail how to select your lawyer. By following those recommendations, you will be able to select an attorney who will assemble your "dream team" to help you navigate your divorce case. At the conclusion of your case, as you transition into working primarily with your wealth management team, you may add additional members to your team as the divorce lawyer's role ends. Please make sure your lawyer and/or wealth management team will be able to connect you with the best professionals to help you achieve your financial goals.

We gave our client Laura this same advice. Laura is a public schoolteacher and is twelve years younger than Ron, a real estate investor who owned one of Palm

Beach's top boutique hotels. When Laura and Ron's marriage fell apart after twenty years, she was extremely concerned about how she would provide for her two sons and have sufficient monthly income to live on her own. She's always depended on Ron to provide financially for the family.

We helped Laura and her lawyer form a team of successful professionals who were as knowledgeable as they were loyal. We told her to do what all CEOs do, which is to surround themselves with the most competent people they can find. Do you think Bill and Melinda Gates manage their own money? No. Most successful people know they need team players who can counter their weaknesses. Not one person on the new team Laura assembled came from the advisors she and Ron used during her married life.

Shortly after her divorce, Laura came into our office for one of her regularly scheduled review meetings. She was adjusting well to life on her own and becoming more comfortable handling the finances. Eighteen months later, when she came back again, we could not believe we were talking to the same person we had met at the beginning of her divorce. Laura was excited about life; she had a new boyfriend and enjoyed new hobbies. She is still working as a teacher and was able to buy her own house—with three bedrooms for her sons to use when they come home from college.

WHAT'S IMPORTANT IS THE PRESENT

At this critical turning point in your life, it is important not to beat yourself up. Questions we often hear our clients asking themselves include, "How could I not have been involved with our finances?" or "Why was I so naive?" Remember, though, that when people get married, they function as a team. They divide their duties, jobs, and roles. In many cases, women take care of the home and children.

Even a financially literate woman can find herself in a situation in which she never could have imagined. One of our clients, Debbie, was the practice manager for a large Jacksonville law firm. Her husband, Rick, had a successful orthodontics practice. Debbie and Rick enjoyed an extravagant lifestyle. While assisting Debbie and her lawyer with the couple's divorce case, we helped identify thousands of dollars of personal expenses and gifts that Rick had purchased for his girlfriend. Not only that, but he had financed them through his orthodontics practice. Because Debbie had always trusted Rick, she never thought twice about looking through his practice's financial records. Having experts who were skilled in spotting these types of issues added necessary expertise to Debbie's case.

If you can't stop ruminating that here you are getting divorced and you have no idea what your assets are, then step back from that runaway train of thought. Financial literacy is still rarely taught in school, even in college, which means a tremendous number of adults are not educated in basic finance. If you don't know what compounding means, or what a 401(k) plan is, or how to accurately assess a *rate of return* on an investment, you're not alone. Your team of experts should be able to help you demystify and understand your finances. Your wealth management team is responsible for educating you on your financial matters, both during and following your divorce. This is one of our primary goals with all of our clients who are in your situation. Place your trust in your team of professionals to do their jobs, and know that you will be in good hands.

TENETS OF THIS BOOK

As we said in the beginning, this is a guidebook designed to make a complex financial journey as simple and easy to understand as possible. The book's tenets are:

1. Assemble a team of competent advisors who regularly communicate with you and each other.
2. Have a written plan.
3. Keep the process as simple as possible.
4. Be an optimist; everything is going to work out.

Assemble a team of competent advisors who commu-

nicate with you and each other. The importance of step number one, assembling an all-star team of advisors, has already been discussed. Their responsibilities should be clearly identified in your plan. For example, you may need a CPA or forensic accountant to examine a corporation's books to ascertain if personal expenses are being paid for by your husband's business, as well as what the tax consequences are of the financial transactions performed by you and/or your husband.

Have a written plan. When our client Jan first came to us, she did not have a written plan to help manage her divorce. As a result, her case was stretching out month after month with no end in sight. Attorneys' fees were piling up. Jan was under constant stress. She was receiving temporary alimony, but it was insufficient to meet her needs. Because there were no deadlines and the case was not yet set for trial, she and her case continued to languish. She had no idea she had the right to request that the judge set deadlines for the timely completion of her case. Unfortunately, her lawyer never discussed a case management plan with her either.

Early on in your professional relationship with your lawyer, you should develop a case plan for the efficient and successful completion of your case. A case management order outlines a schedule for each party's attorney that designates deadlines for such matters as *discovery*, *mediation*, the pretrial conference, and the trial itself. (Note: we'll go into more detail in discussing each of these stages throughout the rest of the book.) The written plan for your case should be comprehensive and should include the evidence and testimony you will need to provide the court to prove your case. With a written, detailed plan, nothing falls through the cracks and no surprises surface after the conclusion of the divorce. Plus, the plan keeps everyone accountable and ensures that your case is progressing toward completion.

It is easier to grasp the importance of a solid plan when you think about the blueprint and the plan for building a house. Before anything can happen, the site must first be prepped and graded. Next comes the foundation. You cannot install electrical and plumbing if there is no roof. Without a plan for what needs to happen and when, the entire process is haphazard, and the contractors have both a blank check and the ability to come and go as they please. Similarly, a written plan for your divorce designates a schedule for critical milestones such as discovery, *depositions*, and determining which experts may need to be involved. A plan also helps keep a lid on the amount of money you are or might be spending on attorney's fees. The plan may evolve as the case progresses or when new information or circumstances may dictate a change to the plan.

Keep the process as simple as possible. The third tenet

of this book is to keep the plan—and the overall divorce process—as simple as possible. Keeping things simple for the court or for a mediation conference entails, for example, using an easy-to-understand chart or a clearly written one-page summary. It's important to remember most judges and *mediators* aren't financial experts. As a result, everyone with whom you are interacting must understand what you're trying to convey. If evidence is overwhelmingly complex, or if you have an expert who cannot succinctly and effectively explain a matter to a judge, your position will suffer.

Be an optimist; everything is going to work out as it should. Make optimism a daily practice—you must avoid falling into an abyss of pessimism. We added this tenet at the suggestion of one of our clients who recently concluded her case and suggested we add a section on how to "conduct" yourself during the case. Going through a divorce is like navigating a foreign country. Without the ability to communicate in a foreign country, travel would be overwhelming. Alongside your team of advisors, it often helps to have a best friend and confidant to help you through the tougher times.

In a divorce setting, fears of loss abound: loss of status, social networks, lifestyle, companionship, and the ability to go on vacations, just to name several. However, fear about the future is often misguided. Although lifestyles may have to change to some degree, the vast majority of our clients' fears usually pass in short order. It may be hard to believe, but many clients are happier after their divorces than they have ever been in their lives.

Following the four tenets described above will provide you with a much more efficient and predictable divorce case. This will become clearer as you continue reading this book. A competent team should be skilled and precise in their work. Having a plan will hold everyone on the team accountable to their clearly defined roles. Keeping the process as simple as possible will eliminate unnecessary confusion. Staying optimistic will allow you to prioritize what truly matters and prevent you from wasting time on issues that have no significance to achieving your ultimate goals.

THE VALUE OF SHERPAS

Even with the most competent divorce attorney, our clients often have questions that they are reluctant to ask their lawyers (who bill by the hour). Lawyers, for their part, are often busy with many cases and are not trained in finance. Many attorneys see their role as simply dividing the "marital pie" in such a way that you will receive as much of it as possible. As a result, attorney-client communication (or lack thereof) sometimes gets lost in the process.

Our clients want to and should be educated about their divorce process. They want to understand the reasons for each action and know what to expect to come next. One of Pat's clients recently shared with him the following perspective: "I found the lack of contact with my lawyer to be the *most* frustrating aspect of my divorce." We aim to eliminate this frustration for our clients.

We think of ourselves as Sherpa guides for our clients going through a divorce. Specifically, we are experienced guides, familiar with the terrain who can make the divorce journey far easier for our clients. By having Pat on our team, we are able to fill in some of the "understanding" gaps for our clients that their lawyer may overlook or not identify. Although Pat is not giving our clients legal advice, he does spend time explaining the process, documents, and strategy with our clients. Further, he often helps our clients assemble the various financial documents that their lawyers request, and provides expert witness testimony, when necessary. With a competent team of advisors by your side, you can be confident in your journey forward.

CHAPTER TWO

Which Attorney Should You Hire?

The first stage of a divorce occurs when the papers are filed with the clerk of the court by either you or your husband. If your husband files, the normal procedure is that a process server knocks on your door and hands you the papers. You now have twenty days to obtain an attorney and respond. When the case is filed, a judge is assigned to your case. Most clients want to "dive in" and immediately hire an attorney. It is important, however, to take sufficient time to select the best attorney for you. The best way to identify a compatible attorney is through an unbiased recommendation from someone with a deep understanding of the divorce process and who has a strong network with divorce attorneys and other professionals in your local area.

In our office, Pat acts as that "referral source" for our clients. His previous experience as a family law attorney in Northeast Florida enables him to help our clients identify attorneys with the right expertise and personality fit. In addition, he knows the local landscape of judges, mediators, and potential experts who might be beneficial to your case.

DON'T FLY SOLO

You might think you can go through the process of getting a divorce without using attorneys. Many people believe this, especially couples who have made the decision to remain friends, despite ending their marriage. Unfortunately, not having competent legal representation usually fails to work out, often leading to more delays, greater costs, and catastrophic financial mistakes and surprises.

Diane came to us after trying to navigate a divorce from her husband, John, without an attorney. John had built a successful advertising business in Northeast Florida, and the couple owned a multimillion-dollar home overlooking the St. Johns River. When John and Diane decided to part amicably, John moved in with his girlfriend. Diane stayed in the original family home, and John agreed to pay all of the bills. They also committed to spending holidays together with their college-age son, Nick.

Three years later, they were still married despite Diane's best efforts to get John to compromise on a number of issues. He kept postponing one meeting after another. John eventually agreed to pay for an attorney to represent him and draft settlement documents. (Note: it is a conflict of interest to have one attorney represent both parties.) Diane reluctantly agreed to allow John's attorney to draft the documents, but another year passed with no substantial movement. Diane began to feel trapped. In addition, when it came time to conduct a valuation of John's advertising business, Diane was concerned about getting an accurate assessment. She was also worried about getting her fair share of the couple's substantial retirement plan. She finally came to us at this juncture.

We recommended to Diane that if she wanted to get divorced within the next millennium, she must hire her own lawyer. Enough was enough. We gave her a list of candidates, and Diane hired an excellent attorney using the "Guide for Interviewing an Attorney" provided later in this chapter.

When each person is represented by an attorney and has a plan with deadlines in place, the divorce case moves along more timely and efficiently. Keep in mind that there is an opportunity cost to unnecessarily dragging out a divorce: marital assets can be significantly affected. While John and Diane's case dragged on, the value of their home plummeted. In addition, long delays without attorneys involved can also create the opportunity for assets to be hidden or wasted. These are but two examples of financial catastrophes that we have seen when women trust their estranged husbands to not involve attorneys in the process.

You should hire an attorney whom you will respect and trust to lead you to your ultimate goals. There are going to be many issues that you, your friends, and/or your family believe to be extremely relevant that end up being totally insignificant to the ultimate resolution of your case. You will need to trust your lawyer and listen to his or her advice above all else. Abraham Lincoln once said, "He who serves as his own counsel has a fool for a lawyer and a jackass for a client."

DUE DILIGENCE IS ESSENTIAL

Movies and television often portray divorce attorneys as bulldogs or icy, cutthroat professionals. Our advice: don't assume you need an attorney with those characteristics. What you do need is an individual who is competent, professional, honest, prepared, strategic, and service-oriented (i.e., returns your phone calls and keeps you regularly updated).

We recognize that selecting an appropriate attorney is especially difficult when navigating one of the most emotionally draining and financially significant experiences of your life. More than one client has told us that going through a divorce was so exhausting that at times she didn't even want to get out of bed in the morning.

Take your time when selecting an attorney. This should be one of the least impulse-driven decisions you ever make. Don't automatically go on a friend's recommendation or a secondhand referral. Most importantly, do not let your spouse force you to retain a certain lawyer. They may have ulterior motives in pushing you to use the lawyer they are suggesting. For example, they might be suggesting you use a less expensive attorney because they know that lawyer will not be as skilled/experienced as their lawyer on tax issues.

Do your homework like you would when buying a house. You might love a home's newly remodeled interior, but without an inspection you won't know whether the home is structurally sound. If not, the roof could cave in during a severe storm or the air conditioner may be at the end of its functional life. When evaluating an attorney, keep in mind that their job is to take charge of your case, not take care of your emotions. Your emotions are the domain of a therapist. It is not the lawyer's job to be your friend either. We advise you to look for a good personality fit, but don't discount an excellent attorney if they aren't as warm as you'd like.

If you come to the conclusion that your lawyer is not the one to handle your case, it is OK to switch. There will be some expenses associated with catching the new lawyer up to speed on your case, but that expense will be outweighed by the significant harm you could endure by sticking with the wrong lawyer. In our experience, you should try to avoid changing lawyers during your case more than once. Although there is no limit to the number of times you can change lawyers, at some point, it will unnecessarily prolong the case, and if there are several changes, the judge may perceive you to be the problem.

Unfortunately, a number of law firms that currently market their services on television, radio, and the internet do so with a powerful figurehead who gives the impression that they will be your sole attorney. But when clients retain such a firm, they are frequently dismayed to discover they've been assigned to an associate with substantially less experience. One of the dangers in this scenario is that during such an emotional and exhausting time, many people will be tempted to simply stick with the attorney to whom they have been assigned, instead of insisting on what they really need: an experienced professional who is skilled in many of the issues a high-net-worth divorce presents. The bottom line is that due diligence is absolutely vital.

A PROCESS OF MATCHMAKING

The process of hiring an attorney is similar to matchmaking. One of the first things we do is ask our clients about their primary objectives. Is it to maximize time with their children? Is it to protect them, if necessary, from an abusive spouse? Is it to obtain a fair and equitable share of her spouse's business?

Next, we focus on narrowing down the choices for an attorney. Some lawyers who have been practicing for decades are no longer interested in custody cases but are excellent litigators of sophisticated financial cases. A number of attorneys specialize in domestic violence cases or those involving substance abuse. Others excel in business valuation cases. You need an attorney with the skills required to address your specific circumstances with a track record of achieving the desired results in similar cases. Such individuals do exist, and you can find the right person to represent you.

Meanwhile, judges often have specific ways that their individual courtrooms are run. For example, the family law judges in Florida's St. Johns County, southeast of Jacksonville, hold a quarterly meeting called the Family Law Advisory Group (FLAG). Each quarter, the judges expect all the family law attorneys, mediators, and *expert witnesses* who practice in their courts to attend to learn the rules and preferences for their courtroom. Attendees also make suggestions on how to improve the court system. Having a lawyer with significant courtroom experience in your county will be to your benefit.

From county to county, local rules and preferences change, and an experienced attorney will understand these nuances. In addition, the power of institutional memory cannot be underestimated. An experienced attorney will know your judge's tendencies, the opposing attorney's tendencies, where the judge went to law school, and so on. Underlying every different court system and county are people and their interconnected web of relationships and perspectives.

We strive to act as a support system by helping our clients select attorneys who will educate them on the law regarding their specific issues and objectives, as well as set realistic expectations at every stage of the case.

GUIDE FOR INTERVIEWING AN ATTORNEY

Attorneys and clients rarely run into problems in their professional relationships over legal matters. Conflicts instead usually arise because expectations were not made clear in the beginning about the level of service a client wants and needs, and whether the attorney is able to provide it. These expectations should be discussed in the initial meeting. We recommend interviewing at least three attorneys using the checklist provided below. Be prepared to pay a consultation fee ranging from $350 to $500 or more for each meeting. That may sound pricey, but an excellent attorney will potentially save you a great deal of money in your divorce case.

A good law office will provide the basic information upon your first phone call, including the following:

- The price of the consultation fee and required retainer.

- Available payment methods and how fees are typically incurred.

- Length of the first meeting and required materials.

- Office location.

Questions to ask during your meeting include (among others):

1. Who is ultimately going to be in charge of setting the vision and strategy for my case?

2. Do you have enough time to devote to handling my case?

3. Will you be creating a divorce plan, and will it contain deadlines?

4. How many people work in your office, and what role will they play in my divorce case?

5. Do you have any former clients whom I can contact as references?

6. What is the best method of communication, and who will be returning my inquiries and answering my specific questions?

7. How quickly will my emails/phone calls/texts be answered?

8. How will most of our conversations happen? In person or by phone?

9. What is your hourly rate? What is your retainer fee? Is your retainer refundable? Do I have to replenish my retainer?

10. How do I reach you in an emergency situation?

11. What is the typical timeline for scheduling mediation and a trial date?

12. What percentage of your cases settle at mediation?

13. What is your experience with my judge?

14. Do you have experience working cases with my specific set of facts? Please discuss these general outcomes.

15. Do you have a group of expert witnesses whom you work with regularly?

16. From a high-level perspective, how do you envision the strategy of my case?

EVERY JUDGE IS DIFFERENT

Although the law is the law, interpreting and upholding laws is performed by human beings whose unique perspectives and biases factor into their decisions. This may not sound entirely fair, but it is the reality of the situation. Judge Stanley, for example, is in his early sixties. He grew up in a two-parent household where his father worked full time in an office and his mother stayed home and took care of him and his sister. His upbringing shapes his views about how children should be raised. In custody cases, Judge Stanley trends toward awarding majority *timesharing* to the mother.

On the other hand, Judge Johnson is a male judge in his early forties whose views were shaped in part by the women's movement. He trends toward an equitable perspective when it comes to parenting. Judge Johnson is more likely to consider timesharing arrangements that are equally divided between both parents.

In sum, every judge is different. In Florida, family law judges have a tremendous amount of discretion on a number of issues. Consequently, it is critical you hire a lawyer familiar with your particular judge. A strong understanding of your judge's background and judicial philosophy will be beneficial in preparing your case.

For example, in alimony cases under Florida law, judges

have full discretion to determine whether one party has a need and whether the other party has the ability to pay for alimony. Although judges are bound by evidence, they are enabled to make decisions on which expenses are luxuries and which are necessities. Knowing in advance where your judge may stand on this spectrum is valuable information.

A circuit judge in the state of Florida earns a salary of approximately $160,000 per year (as of 2020). If a woman who does not work outside the home requests $350,000 per year in alimony from a Florida family law judge when the husband argues she needs only $250,000 per year, it is critical to provide the court with compelling and concrete reasons for requesting the higher amount. The judge will likely feel little empathy for a person who rejects an offer substantially more than the judge's own salary. If your attorney is familiar with your judge, however, he or she may be in a better position to present such a request so it is more likely to be awarded.

In sum, the importance of the attorney-judge connection cannot be underestimated. When it comes to your case, their relationship is, in many ways, like two sides of a coin. You can't separate one from the other.

ACTION ITEMS

To select the best legal representative for your case, adhere to the following guidelines:

- Obtain recommendations of at least three divorce attorneys from someone with a strong network of relevant professionals specific to where you live.
- Research the backgrounds of each attorney and check references.
- Conduct initial consultations with at least two or three attorneys before finalizing your selection. (Don't worry so much about the initial consultation fee. Making a bad decision will cost you more than the consultation fee in the end.)
- Use the "Guide for Interviewing an Attorney" during your search.
- Verify that the attorney whom you hire has significant experience practicing in the courts where you live (because every judge is different), is well-respected, and possesses the required expertise.
- Confirm communication expectations up front. The number one complaint we hear from our clients about lawyers is that they are not always available for their client. At the first meeting, determine how you are going to work with your lawyer to avoid similar issues.
- Hire an attorney! Do not go through your case unrepresented!

Now that we have discussed the best practices for hiring a compatible and competent attorney, we will next focus on the step-by-step breakdown of the divorce process. Having an understanding of the overall divorce process can enable you to navigate this journey in a more confident and manageable manner.

CHAPTER THREE

Breakdown of a Divorce Case

Every divorce is different, each with its own level of complexity. In this chapter, we will provide an overview of the divorce process and outline the primary five steps: the initial steps, discovery, temporary needs, mediation and informal settlement negotiations, and the final judgment or trial. If necessary, there may also be an appeal.

If you do nothing else throughout this process, hire a competent attorney to represent you. It is the number one way to help you achieve the desired outcome. Many people try to represent themselves in their divorce case. In fact, 73 percent of all divorce cases in Florida's largest counties have at least one party representing themselves.[2] As an analogy, many people assume they can follow YouTube videos to learn how to do electrical work on their homes. Unfortunately, they may end up starting a fire or electrocuting themselves, at which point they will regret not hiring a professional. It is not so different when it comes to divorce.

THE DIVORCE PROCESS

Let's walk through several stages of the divorce process through the eyes of a couple in Northeast Florida: Christine and Joseph. The couple lives in Atlantic Beach and

DEADLINES ARE ESSENTIAL

Just like applying for college, a successful divorce cannot be successfully navigated without deadlines. Specifically, deadlines must be set for completing discovery, furnishing expert reports, and setting a trial. Your attorney is the quarterback when it comes to setting deadlines. From the point at which the divorce case is filed to the time of the mediation conference, the timetable for completion in a best-case scenario is approximately six months. Again, you wouldn't build a house without a blueprint, right? Well, you shouldn't begin your divorce case without a "blueprint," complete with deadlines along the way.

---

2 Madelynn Herman, "Self-Representation: Pro Se Statistics," National Center for State Courts, September 25, 2006, https://web.archive.org/web/20120504035215/ and http:/www.ncsconline.org/wc/publications/memos/prosestatsmemo.htm from 2012-05-04.

has been married for twelve years. Joseph is the primary wage earner, while Christine has tended to the home and their son, Eli. Repeated disagreements over money have led to the divorce.

THE DIVORCE PROCESS

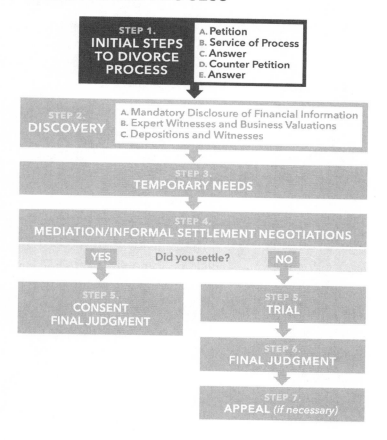

1. THE PETITIONER AND RESPONDENT

Joseph initiates the process by filing a *petition* for dissolution of marriage. Hence, Joseph is the *petitioner*. Christine receives the document via service of process (meaning the papers are legally delivered), and by being last in that role, she is known as the *respondent*.

Joseph's petition outlines his requests to the court for relief. Because Joseph has been the breadwinner, he doesn't ask for alimony in his petition. However, he does ask for *equitable distribution*—which, as we will discuss in more detail, is the fair division of all the marital assets and liabilities that each party acquired individually or in their joint names during their marriage. Because Eli is a minor, Joseph asks the court to award him a timesharing arrangement with Eli, as well as other requests.

Under Florida law, Christine now has twenty days to respond to Joseph with what is called the respondent's *answer to the petition for dissolution of marriage*. Her lawyer will file this document on her behalf. Christine's answer goes through each paragraph of Joseph's petition and either admits or denies each allegation he makes. Even though Joseph filed the petition first, Christine is allowed to file her own petition (counter petition; see image) outlining her requests for relief to the court. She, too, requests a specific timesharing arrangement with Eli, as well as an equitable distribution of the marital assets and liabilities. In addition, Christine requests alimony and an award of attorney's fees from Joseph. She also asks for Joseph to provide health insurance for her and Eli, as well as pay for any medical costs insurance does not cover. In addition, she will ask for child support and for the court to require Joseph to secure adequate life insurance policies with a sufficient death benefit to secure any alimony and child support awarded.

It's important to understand that at this stage, whether you file the initial petition or whether you're the respondent, you need to ask the court for everything you want. Just because you ask does not mean you're going to get it. But if you don't ask, the court can't award it to you.

When Joseph is served with Christine's counter petition, he has ten days to respond (answer). In sum, both the respondent and the petitioner have a reciprocal obligation to file an answer or response to the other party's petition.

We are frequently asked if Christine (or someone in her situation) would be disadvantaged in any way because Joseph "won the race to the courthouse" and filed his petition first. The answer is essentially no. If Joseph and Christine's case had to go to trial because they were unable to settle it with the help of a mediator, Joseph would present his case first. However, both sides would have an equal amount of time to present their case to the judge.

THE DIVORCE PROCESS

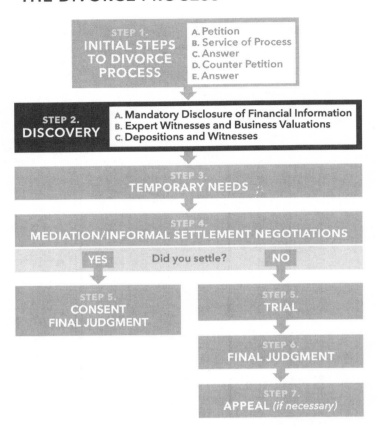

2. DISCOVERY

Discovery of financial information is a necessary part of every divorce case. It is the relevant financial information each party collects in order to settle or try the case. Specifically, discovery includes bank, credit card, and investment statements; depositions; reports from expert witnesses; and appraisals and valuations of businesses.

Discovery comprises the evidential pieces of the puzzle required for the mediator and/or judge to see the entire picture.

One of the most essential components of discovery is the mandatory disclosure of financial information. *Mandatory disclosure documents* are made up of sixteen items that both parties are automatically required to produce in all Florida divorce cases. Within forty-five days of the filing date of the original divorce petition, both Joseph and Christine have a reciprocal obligation to provide each other with mandatory financial discovery. Although the mandatory disclosure documents are automatically required to be produced as part of the divorce process, your attorney has the right to request additional documents. Odds are, more documents will be requested. As mediation and/or trial approach, you might be requested to provide updated documents and statements.

If this is your first time looking at this list, you might feel completely overwhelmed. Clients have reported to us, especially at the beginning of the case, that they felt gathering all of these documents was a full-time job. However, this process is a necessary evil.

MANDATORY DISCLOSURE DOCUMENTS

Below are the sixteen items that comprise the mandatory disclosure documents, as outlined in the Florida Family Law Rules of Procedure:[3]

1. A *financial affidavit*.

2. All federal and state income tax returns, gift tax returns, and intangible property-tax returns filed by the party or on the party's behalf for the past three years.

3. IRS forms W-2, 1099, and K-1 for the past year, if the income tax return for that year has not been prepared.

4. Pay stubs or other evidence of earned income for the three months prior to service of the financial affidavit.

5. A statement by the producing party identifying the amount and source of all income received from any source during the three months preceding the service of the financial affidavit, if not reflected on the pay stubs produced.

6. All loan applications and financial statements prepared or used within the twelve months preceding service of that party's financial affidavit, whether for the purpose of obtaining or attempting to obtain credit or for any other purpose.

7. All deeds within the last three years, all promissory notes within the last twelve months, and all present leases in which the party owns or owned an interest, whether held in the party's name individually, in the party's name jointly with any other person or entity, in the party's name as *trustee* or guardian for any other person, or in someone else's name on the party's behalf.

8. All statements from the last three months for all checking accounts, and from the last twelve months for all other accounts (for example, savings accounts, money market funds, certificates of deposit, etc.), regardless of whether or not the account has been closed, including those held in the party's name individually, in the party's name jointly with any other person or entity, in the party's name as trustee or guardian for any other person, or in someone else's name on the party's behalf.

9. All brokerage account statements and/or college savings account statements in which either party to this action held within the last twelve months or holds an interest, including those held in the party's name individually, in the party's name jointly with any person or entity, in the party's name as trustee or guardian for any other person, or in someone else's name on the party's behalf.

10. The most recent statement for any profit sharing, retirement, deferred compensation, or pension plan (for example, IRA, 401(k), *403(b)*, SEP, KEOGH, or other similar account) in which the party is a participant or alternate payee and the summary plan description for any retirement, profit sharing, or pension plan in which the party is a participant or an alternate payee.

11. The declarations page, the last periodic statement, and the certificate for all life insurance policies insuring the party's life or the life of the party's spouse, whether group insurance or otherwise, and all current health and dental insurance cards covering either of the parties and/or their dependent children.

12. Corporate, partnership, and trust tax returns for the last three tax years if the party has an ownership or interest in a corporation, partnership, or trust greater than or equal to 30 percent.

13. All promissory notes for the last twelve months, all credit card and charge account statements and other records showing the party's indebtedness as of the date of the filing of this action and for the last three months, and all present lease agreements, whether owed in the party's name individually, in the party's name jointly with any other person or entity, in the party's name as trustee or guardian for any other person, or in someone else's name on the party's behalf.

14. All written premarital or marital agreements entered into at any time between the parties to this marriage, whether before or during the marriage.

15. All documents and tangible evidence supporting the producing party's claim of the nonmarital status of an asset or debt for the time period from the date of acquisition of the asset or debt to the date of production or from the date of marriage, if based on premarital acquisition.

16. Any court orders directing a party to pay or receive spousal or child support.

The first item on the list of mandatory disclosure documents is the financial affidavit. Think of it as the summary of the information reflected in the mandatory disclosure documents. The financial affidavit is a list of each person's sources of monthly income and expenses, all assets and the estimated value of those assets, and any liabilities

---

3   Rule 12.285 (d)(1-16) of the Florida Family Law Rules of Procedure, https://www. floridasupremecourt.org/content/download/345287/3052131/01-2344_rule.pdf.

and their current balances. This document is arguably the most important document in the entire divorce case.

In Florida, a financial affidavit is a ten-page form. (To see what one looks like, go to www.divorceadv.com/financial-affidavit.) Because it is a legal document, accuracy is essential, and you and your husband are expected to complete the affidavit to the best of your ability, under penalty of perjury. Because of its complexity, most people feel overwhelmed upon viewing a financial affidavit for the first time. Often, they don't know what to do if they don't possess all the information and are at a loss as to how to obtain it. They can be confused about how to complete the form if there is a need to explain financial information in more detail.

Confusion also arises if a spouse's affidavit is inaccurate. Often, information needed to complete the affidavit is not part of the required mandatory financial disclosure documents. Here is where a Certified Divorce Financial Analyst™ may be an enormous help. This expert advisor is familiar with the process and can usually assist in nearly every way, from helping to collect the information to explaining each detail to the client. On a financial affidavit, the more detail you provide, the better; footnotes are an excellent tool for you to add in order to explain specific entries. Further, an obligation exists for both parties to update the affidavit if a significant change occurs in one of the four areas (income, expenses, assets, and liabilities) or in the event of a mistake. For example, if during the divorce, your husband receives a high-level promotion with a significant increase in income, his affidavit must be amended. If you receive an inheritance after you file your affidavit, you should file a new financial affidavit disclosing the inherited funds.

To understand how the affidavit and the rest of the mandatory disclosure documents dovetail to provide a complete financial picture for the court, think of a painting where you connect the dots. The affidavit provides the dots: the income, expenses, assets, and liabilities. The rest of the documents—from bank statements to pay stubs—color in the painting to construct a complete financial picture.

The other mandatory disclosure documents are requested because they support the information listed on the financial affidavit. For example, tax returns can serve many purposes, such as verifying wages from employment. Additionally, the dividends and interest sections may identify assets that may have not been reported on the financial affidavit. If your spouse owns a business, the tax return will provide information on business expenses, along with many other pieces of valuable information.

Expert Witnesses and Business Valuations

For some assets, you and your husband may agree on their value. Other assets, such as the value of a business, may need professional assistance in order for you to ascertain their values.

An *expert witness* is a professional who has a certain expertise that will help the court understand a specific issue or help arrive at the value of an asset. These experts will generally prepare a report of their work. This work is then typically shared with your husband and his attorney. To prepare for mediation or a court hearing, the opposing attorney may want to take the expert witness's *deposition* to ask the expert about their methodology, the sources of information that they considered in preparing their report, and their conclusions.

For example, you and your husband may have established a business during your marriage. Unlike a house where you can go on a website like Zillow.com and get a sense of the value, you may need an expert—in this case, a business valuator—to help you place a value on the business within the context of your divorce case. Business valuations will be discussed in Chapter 7.

This information is helpful when trying to settle your case, or to the court if settlement does not occur. As you can see, experts are an integral part of the discovery process.

Depositions and Witnesses

Because every divorce is unique, so are its discovery parameters. In some divorce cases (very few), there's no need for discovery. Everyone is credible, the case is not financially complex, and each party simply provides the necessary financial documents.

In other divorces, less cooperative or less credible parties are involved, and witnesses and depositions are required. Depositions of those witnesses are additional discovery or additional "dots." By formal definition, a deposition is a witness's sworn, out-of-court testimony (transcribed by a court reporter), which may be used in court or for the purposes of further discovery.

In simpler terms, depositions are taken when a person has information relevant to the divorce case. In Joseph and Christine's case, for example, Christine was concerned about the decline in Joseph's K-1 distributions (as shown on his *Schedule K-1*) from his company. She was concerned Joseph was hiding some of his income. Her lawyer subsequently subpoenaed Joseph's company's Chief Financial Officer to answer questions under oath that Christine and her lawyer had relating to Joseph's compensation.

If you request that a deposition of a party or witness be taken, you are entitled to be present, but it's not a requirement. However, it can be important for you to be there.

You might remember circumstances differently from the witness being deposed, or want your attorney to ask follow-up questions on a specific point. During a deposition, you can pass a note to your attorney requesting that he or she ask the witness for clarification or more detail. Examples of people who could be deposed as a witness include employers, neighbors, CPAs, business valuators, and anyone who may have relevant information about your case.

Specific rules govern depositions. It is standard that each party has their own lawyer present to ensure the deposition is being conducted fairly and professionally.

THE DIVORCE PROCESS

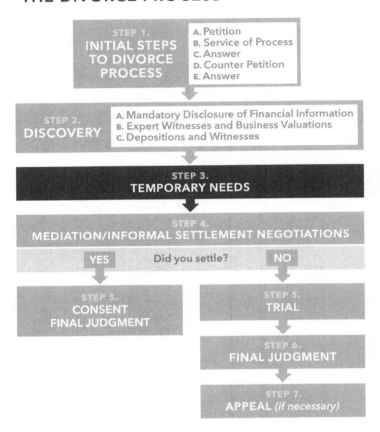

STEP 1.
INITIAL STEPS TO DIVORCE PROCESS
A. Petition
B. Service of Process
C. Answer
D. Counter Petition
E. Answer

STEP 2.
DISCOVERY
A. Mandatory Disclosure of Financial Information
B. Expert Witnesses and Business Valuations
C. Depositions and Witnesses

STEP 3.
TEMPORARY NEEDS

STEP 4.
MEDIATION/INFORMAL SETTLEMENT NEGOTIATIONS

YES Did you settle? NO

STEP 5.
CONSENT FINAL JUDGMENT

STEP 5.
TRIAL

STEP 6.
FINAL JUDGMENT

STEP 7.
APPEAL *(if necessary)*

3. TEMPORARY NEEDS

Up to this point, we have assumed both Christine and Joseph will have access to money to hire their own attorney and be relatively cooperative with each other. Unfortunately, this is not always the case.

What happens if your husband files for divorce and eliminates your access to your checking and savings accounts? How do you get access to funds to hire a lawyer? If this is the situation you are facing, you will need to notify your lawyer immediately. They will usually make arrangements with you until you regain access to your accounts to pay their retainer fee.

In Florida, your lawyer will be able to request what's called a temporary needs hearing. At this hearing, the court will make temporary arrangements for custody/timesharing arrangements with children, alimony, child support, and attorney's fee payments. Relative to a trial or a final hearing, this will generally be a much shorter hearing. The court realizes discovery is not complete, and this hearing is set quickly—sometimes within a month of the petition being filed. Further, the court does not want to conduct two trials in the same case.

The purpose of this hearing will be simply to set some initial parameters around timesharing with the children, alimony, child support, and attorneys' and experts' fees. If the court has to decide these issues at a temporary needs hearing, this ruling does not prejudice either party's ultimate claim or position at a final hearing. For example, if you are asking the court to ultimately award you $15,000 per month in alimony, and at a temporary needs hearing the court awards you $12,000 per month in temporary alimony, this will not be held against you if the case ultimately heads to trial. In a temporary needs hearing, the court is simply trying to set some guidelines for timesharing with the children and finances until all the issues are mediated or ruled on by the court following completion of financial discovery.

We have not given this subject much treatment because in high-net-worth cases, each party is typically represented by an experienced attorney, and these temporary issues are often resolved between the lawyers without the necessity of a court hearing.

Let's revisit the previous example of your husband blocking your access to your checking and savings accounts. What happens in practice is that you would generally meet with an attorney, and your attorney would call your husband's attorney to let them know that you are being denied access to funds to retain a lawyer. Your husband's lawyer likely does not know this is happening. They will then call your husband and advise him to make appropriate funds available to you. Your husband's lawyer will not want the judge's first impression of their client (your estranged husband) to be that of a person trying to financially suffocate you by denying you access to sufficient funds while the case is pending.

The most important thing to remember about this section is that the judge will not let your spouse call the shots with regard to the finances while the case is pending. However, it is more efficient and economical if you can reach an agreement internally, rather than relying on your judge to make rulings on these temporary issues.

THE DIVORCE PROCESS

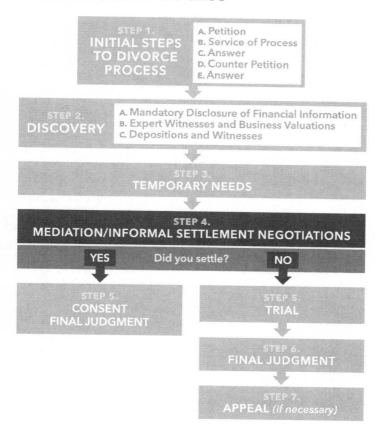

4. MEDIATION/INFORMAL SETTLEMENT NEGOTIATION

When discovery is completed, mediation is the next step (we will discuss the process in detail in Chapter 5). *Mediation* is an informal, confidential conference used by a couple to attempt to amicably settle all or part of the issues in their divorce case. You generally do not want to attempt mediation until you have sufficient information needed to make you feel ready to negotiate.

It is important to note that your case can settle at any time. A number of cases reach a conclusion after the lawyers negotiate a settlement directly without the assistance of a mediator. Sometimes a settlement is negotiated through written correspondence going back and forth between the lawyers. In Florida, if your case has not settled before you go to trial, the court requires you to attend a mediation conference before the court will set your case for trial. Please know that over 90 percent of divorce cases settle without the court having to get involved to perform a detailed probe of your family and finances.

The *mediator* is a neutral third party whose goal is to try to help you and your husband reach an amicable resolution. Mediation is a confidential process. When you appear in front of the judge (assuming mediation did not result in a settlement), he or she will not know what communications took place during the mediation conference; hence, nothing that happens in mediation can be used against you or for you in court or in any other way.

Certified family law mediators can be attorneys as well, but one of the most important things for you to know is that it is not the mediator's role to provide legal advice. That is why you should hire a competent attorney. We strongly advise against participating in the mediation process without the guidance of your attorney.

Because the vast majority of cases settle at mediation, we cannot emphasize enough the importance of preparing for the mediation conference. This is arguably the most important day of your whole case. Making sure you have as much information as you need to make an informed decision is essential! Do not feel like you need to go into the mediation conference simply because it is scheduled. You can always ask for the mediation conference to be rescheduled. We discuss mediation in much more detail in Chapter 5—just know it is not possible to overprepare for the mediation conference. Even though your lawyer will give you a range of what they think will be a good outcome or a good deal, the ultimate decision on whether to take the deal or not is yours.

It is important to note that even after a divorce, you may be able to modify custody, alimony, and child support agreements. What you cannot modify are the terms relating to the division of your assets and liabilities. In one example, Brad and Sandra handled their divorce on their own, filling out the required forms without attorneys. However, when it came to equitably dividing the assets and liabilities, they did not include the house. They forgot! They had verbally agreed Sandra would get the house, but her mother-in-law, Bev, who was living in it at the time, would be able to continue to do so for a year. After the year ended, Bev refused to leave the residence, and Sandra wanted to start eviction proceedings. Because both Brad's and Sandra's names were still on the home's title, and the marital assets and liabilities had already been divided, the court did not have the ability to go back and address this issue. Sandra was told by her lawyer there was nothing she could do to help because they did not have a provision in their mediated settlement agreement addressing the marital residence. Sandra and Brad were eventually able to resolve the situation on their own because there is nothing the law or a judge could do to help them under Florida law. The bottom line is that if you have anything of any significant value, you need to address it at mediation or the final hearing before the judge, with the assistance of a competent family law attorney.

THE DIVORCE PROCESS

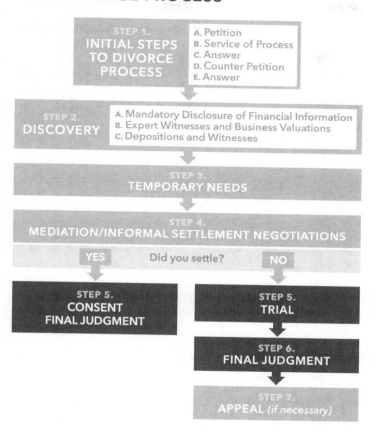

STEP 1.
INITIAL STEPS TO DIVORCE PROCESS
A. Petition
B. Service of Process
C. Answer
D. Counter Petition
E. Answer

STEP 2.
DISCOVERY
A. Mandatory Disclosure of Financial Information
B. Expert Witnesses and Business Valuations
C. Depositions and Witnesses

STEP 3.
TEMPORARY NEEDS

STEP 4.
MEDIATION/INFORMAL SETTLEMENT NEGOTIATIONS

YES — Did you settle? — **NO**

STEP 5.
CONSENT FINAL JUDGMENT

STEP 5.
TRIAL

STEP 6.
FINAL JUDGMENT

STEP 7.
APPEAL *(if necessary)*

5-6. FINAL JUDGMENT AND/OR TRIAL

If your mediation conference is successful, all of the agreements made at mediation will be reduced to writing in an agreement called a mediated settlement agreement. The mediated settlement agreement is then made part of a legal document called a final judgment of dissolution of marriage. Of course, because this agreement was the product of a mediation, this final judgment would be entered (approved) by the court with the consent/agreement of both parties. The judge will be presented with the mediated agreement (now in the form of a consent final judgment) and will sign it as if this was an order that they issued after a trial was conducted.

If mediation is unsuccessful, the way to resolve the ongoing dispute between the parties is through a trial. At the conclusion of the trial, the judge will incorporate their order into a final judgment of dissolution of marriage. This time, this court document will be entered without the consent of the parties. Mediation is extremely advantageous because even though the parties may feel like they are making significant compromises, they are able to make agreements that the court may not necessarily be able to make. Further, the parties are able to include certain provisions into their final judgment that the court may not be able to include, such as enforcement provisions should either party not comply with their agreement. Research shows the parties are more likely to comply with and follow their mediated settlement agreement because they were able to participate in crafting that agreement.[4]

---

4   FindLaw, "Mediation vs. Arbitration vs. Litigation: What's the Difference?" December 2018, https://adr.findlaw.com/mediation/mediation-vs-arbitration-vs-litigation-whats-the-difference.html.

A brief note about a trial. Florida law gives family law judges a tremendous amount of discretion, especially when it comes to the issues of child custody and alimony. A divorce trial in Florida could last for only a few hours or may last as long as several weeks. Once the parties give control to the judge to make the decisions about their lives and future, the results are often unpredictable. Further, a trial is an expensive endeavor. As a rule of thumb, it may take a lawyer two days to prepare for every one day of trial. There are also the costs of preparation and the attendance of all of the expert witnesses who will need to testify at the trial. The emotional toll, expense, and the unpredictability of the outcomes are a few of the many reasons why cases tend to settle at mediation and avoid trial. In sum, mediation is an excellent opportunity for both parties to minimize their attorney's fees, but more importantly, minimize their risks associated with allowing a judge to decide the outcome.

Now that we have discussed the general process and procedure of a divorce case, let's turn our attention to the specific issues you will address in your case.

THE FIVE SUBSTANTIVE ISSUES—PEACE

Although the acronym PEACE can be ironic in the arena of a divorce, it represents five key issues of which you must be aware and the order in which they should be addressed. This book isn't designed to provide legal advice, but we want you to have a general overview of each issue. When it comes to how the following issues relate to your particular divorce case (and especially if you are a resident of a state other than Florida), please consult with your attorney.

P = PARENTAL RESPONSIBILITY

Children are the most significant matter in any divorce case. The two major issues involved with parental responsibility are (1) parental rights and (2) the amount of time each parent will spend with the children, which is called *timesharing* in Florida. In the overwhelming majority of cases, parents agree to have what is called *shared parental responsibility*. It is a court-ordered relationship where both parents continue to enjoy full parental rights and are required to make joint decisions regarding the health, welfare, and education of the children. Regardless of whether the parents get along or remarry, they are required to work together as parents in the best interests of their children. In Florida, each parent's time with the children is detailed in a parenting plan.[5]

In most cases, parents are able to agree on the provisions of a parenting plan. If the parents are not able to agree,

---

5   To see what a parenting plan looks like, visit http://www.flcourts.org/core/fileparse.php/533/urlt/995a.pdf.

the judge will create a parenting plan for the parents. This will involve receiving testimony and evidence about a number of factors that focus on what is best for the children. In some cases where the parenting plan is contested, the judge may appoint a "social investigator" to help give the judge information on what is in the children's best interests. The social investigator could be another family law attorney or even a child psychologist who will spend a considerable amount of time (way more time than the court could ever spend!) meeting with the children, the parents, teachers, healthcare providers, childcare providers, friends, neighbors, and anyone else who has any relevant information about what is in the best interests of the children.

At the conclusion of the social investigator's study, they will prepare a report on their findings and recommendations. This report will be furnished to each party. The social investigator will be called as a witness to testify at trial. The social investigator's testimony will be extremely helpful to the judge. However, the judge must make the final decision. A social investigator generally charges by the hour for their work and court appearances, if necessary. Confirm with your lawyer how a social investigator works in your area and how much a social investigation will likely cost.

E = EQUITABLE DISTRIBUTION

The next issue is dividing the marital assets and liabilities, known as *equitable distribution*. The first step is to classify an asset or liability as either marital or non-marital (your attorney can give you the details on this distinction). Once the marital assets and liabilities are classified and valued, they are then divided. Nonmarital assets are segregated out, and the recipient of the asset maintains ownership. Under Florida law, marital assets and liabilities acquired during the marriage are presumed to be divided equally—unless there is an excellent reason not to do so. An unequal distribution of marital assets and/or liabilities is the exception rather than the rule. If the parties cannot agree on whether an asset is marital or nonmarital, the party seeking to prove an asset is nonmarital has the obligation or burden to prove it is a nonmarital asset.

A = ALIMONY

In Florida, alimony must be determined after the division of the assets. The court determines whether one party has a financial need for alimony and whether the other party has the ability to pay it. If one party has a need but the other party does not have the ability to pay, the court should not order an alimony award.

You might be asking yourself: how does the court determine whether there is a need and/or the ability to pay alimony? It does so by examining the financial affidavit and other relevant documents, which we discussed earlier in this chapter. The affidavit includes two sections that list each party's sources of income and expenses. If the court determines there is a need and an ability to pay, it will consider a number of factors in making an alimony award. The 2020 Statutory Factors are as follows:

- The standard of living established during the marriage
- The length of the marriage
- The age and the physical and emotional condition of each party
- The financial resources of each party, including non-marital and marital assets and liabilities distributed to each
- The earning capacities, educational levels, vocational skills, and employability of the parties, and when applicable, the time necessary for either party to acquire the education or training to enable them to find appropriate employment
- The contribution of each party to the marriage, including but not limited to services rendered in homemaking, childcare, education, and career building of the other party
- The responsibilities each party will have with regard to any minor children they have in common

- The tax treatment and consequences to both parties of any alimony award, including the designation of all or a portion of the payment as a nontaxable, nondeductible payment (As a result of the 2018 federal tax reform law, alimony post-2018 is nontaxable to the recipient and nondeductible by the party paying the alimony)
- All sources of income available to either party, including income available to either party through investments of any asset held by that party
- Any other factor necessary to create equity and justice between the parties

In the past few years, there have been efforts to reform Florida's current alimony law because critics argue that the results are unpredictable and give the court too much discretion. Alimony is an area where you need to rely heavily on your attorney's advice and expertise.

C = CHILD SUPPORT

A child support calculation comes after resolving the timesharing issues, because the number of overnights each parent will spend with each child factors into the calculation. Additionally, a child support determination must follow alimony because each parent's sources of income, including alimony, are taken into consideration in the child support calculation.

Florida law establishes how much support a child needs. The number of children, each parent's monthly income, and a few other factors are input into a legislatively mandated formula to determine each parent's monthly child support obligation. Each parent is responsible for a percentage of the overall financial support of each child. The parent paying child support usually has the higher monthly income. Your lawyer can advise you on how child support will be calculated.

E = EVERYTHING ELSE

Having come this far in your case, you may have particular issues in your case that we haven't addressed. The *E* in PEACE stands for those issues: everything else. They can include matters of domestic violence, mental health, substance abuse, or any other issue, large or small. In family law cases, the major "catchall" issue under this section is attorney's fees.

The issue of attorney's fees is analyzed after the assets are divided, an alimony award is made, and a child support amount has been established because, like alimony, the court's major consideration when considering an attorney's fee is one party's financial need and the other's ability to pay. When the case began, there may have been a tremendous disparity in each party's financial circumstances, but after equitable distribution, alimony, and child support issues are resolved, the parties' financial circumstances may have evened out. Friends may have told you that their husbands were responsible for paying their attorney's fees, but do not automatically assume that will be the case for you. It is extremely important to discuss with your attorney whether you will receive a contribution toward your attorney's fees in your case or not.

In summary, divorce often can be complicated, and preparation is everything. From addressing the five substantive issues of divorce to navigating the mandatory financial disclosure documents, each aspect must be addressed step by step.

ACTION ITEMS

- Hire your attorney as early in the process as possible.
- DO NOT represent yourself in a divorce case.
- Educate yourself on the overall divorce process, paying special attention to the significance of the mediation process.
- Hire someone to help you if you feel overwhelmed by the discovery. It will help eliminate a significant amount of stress.

Now that you have hired your lawyer and have a good overview of the process, procedures, and issues you will encounter, in the next chapter we will discuss how other professionals can assist you and your lawyer to achieve the best possible outcome for your case.

CHAPTER FOUR

Assembling Your Dream Team

In order to take control of your financial future, you need a dream team comprised of competent, loyal people to help you navigate the financial issues of the divorce process and beyond. If you are the breadwinner or have a high-level career, you may already have part or all of this team assembled.

A Chartered Financial Analyst® (CFA®) can be an essential member of such a team. CFA® professionals undergo a rigorous process to gain that certification. It includes passing three increasingly difficult exams and can take several years to complete. The certification also requires a minimum of four years of professional experience. By the time an individual becomes a CFA®, they are extremely knowledgeable in financial, estate, life insurance, tax, retirement, and investment planning in accordance with national standards.

A Certified Public Accountant (CPA) also must pass a series of exams. There are four sections to the exam and they all must be passed within eighteen months. This type of accreditation comes in extremely beneficial when working with complicated business valuations or other accounting matters that often arise in divorce cases.

The path to accreditation for a Certified Divorce Financial Analyst™ (CDFA®) is not as rigorous as that of a CFA®. However, a CDFA® is also a valuable member of your team. In order to receive a CDFA® designation, an individual's course study includes learning divorce procedures and laws as well as the in-depth financial aspects of divorce (including tax issues). A CDFA® must also be knowledgeable of the critical aspects of the negotiation and settlement process. Like a CFA®, a CDFA® must pass several exams and abide by a strict code of ethics. Both of these designations also require continuing professional education.

One of the benefits of having a CDFA® who is also an experienced family law attorney is the added value of legal perspective and experience. They should not dispense actual legal advice, but they can help you navigate divorce-related financial issues and tell you when you need to consult an attorney. Several years ago, one of our clients, Samantha, was getting divorced. The major asset in her case was the value of her share of the staffing company that Samantha and her husband founded during the marriage. During the mediation process, Pat was able to provide his perspective on the legal issues surrounding the different settlement scenarios at the request of Samantha's attorney. Pat's input included answering questions from Samantha's attorney and the mediator, both of whom he knew well from previous cases. Pat's contribution helped to substantially increase the amount that both parties agreed Samantha would receive for her share of the business.

Once you have received the financial discovery (i.e., financial statements, bank records, and taken all necessary depositions), your attorney, a CFA®, a CPA, and a CDFA® can help you navigate your divorce and determine whether other resources are needed.

WHY YOU NEED A DREAM TEAM

Divorce is extremely stressful. Your entire life is changing. A team of trusted advisors is a tremendous source of support, helping you to understand and navigate each step along the way. Team members provide both honesty and perspective. Your divorce lawyer will complete the team that will guide you during the divorce process. Because you have selected an experienced attorney, they will likely know the best litigation support team members to complete your divorce dream team. However, some of these professionals may not remain on your wealth management team once the divorce case concludes because their focus may be limited to litigation support. Here is a brief overview of the typical members on a dream team:

- **Divorce/family law attorney.** They will take charge of your case and guide you through the legal process.
- **Wealth manager.** This professional acts as the captain of the financial aspects of your case, overseeing the big picture of your investments and income, as well as helping to interpret what a settlement might mean in terms of your monthly income and wealth for the future. The wealth manager's job, first and foremost, is to protect your financial security.
- **Certified Public Accountant (CPA)/forensic accountant.** The CPA's role is to assist you in understanding all the tax consequences involved in your divorce and settlement. The forensic accountant is invaluable, particularly when a business is involved. It is their job to help explain the financial data of a marital business, help your lawyer understand each party's lifestyle, and uncover hidden assets, if necessary.
- **Insurance agents.** A property and casualty agent is necessary to help protect all of your assets for which

you have spent so much time negotiating. A life, health, and disability insurance agent's duties include facilitating the securing of your alimony payments as well as protecting you and your family financially in the event you become incapacitated.

- **Estate planning attorney.** This attorney will assist you in changing and/or creating your will, a trust, power of attorney, living will (healthcare surrogate), and ensure the beneficiaries on your retirement plans and insurance policies have been updated where necessary. They will also help coordinate a prenuptial agreement should you remarry.
- **Therapist.** Divorce is one of the most stressful experiences you will endure, and an excellent therapist can help you cope with those overwhelming feelings and emotions. Especially if you have children, a therapist is always a good idea.

ROCK-SOLID SUPPORT

Any wealth management team you hire should go above and beyond to support you. It is not out of the ordinary for such a team to be available to listen to you vent about the stress of the divorce process, provide encouragement when you venture into new work arenas, and help mitigate your fear around stock market volatility.

Above all, look for a team that makes everything as simple

and clear to you as possible. Although financial matters can be confusing at first if you've never before encountered them, nothing is too difficult for you to understand with the right guidance. An excellent lawyer is trained in the law. Most lawyers are not trained as wealth managers, CPAs, insurance professionals, counselors, etc. All of these professionals will add significant and necessary value to your case and help ensure that you will achieve the best possible outcome.

ACTION ITEMS

- Discuss with your lawyer the benefits of having a complete support team to guide and assist you through the divorce process.
- Because each divorce case is factually unique, rely on your team of professionals for advice and expertise—not your friends. Your friends and loved ones mean well but are likely unfamiliar with the facts of your case, the law, your mediator, and your judge.
- At the conclusion of your case, your wealth management plan will already be in place, and you will continue forward with the essential team members who will help you achieve your financial goals.

In the next chapter, we will focus exclusively on the mediation process. Mediation receives its own chapter because the majority of all divorce cases are resolved via mediation. We want you to feel confident in knowing how to prepare for mediation, what to expect when you walk into a mediation conference, and how to prepare for what will be a mentally and emotionally grueling day.

WHAT'S AN INDEPENDENT FIDUCIARY AND WHY DOES IT MATTER?

A financial firm or an individual can act as a fiduciary. An independent fiduciary means that the firm or the individual has a legal obligation to put a client's interests ahead of their own. Our firm is a registered investment advisory firm and an independent fiduciary. Whatever advice we give or product we recommend must be in our client's best interests. Other financial firms exist that operate under a lesser standard called the suitability standard (whose origins go back to the 1940s). Under that standard, a financial firm's duty to their clients is to provide "suitable" investment advice; however, such advice may or may not save the client extra costs or fees. With our independent fiduciary designation, we are held to a much higher standard, dictated by the Securities and Exchange Commission.

An independent fiduciary is the ascendant standard in the financial services industry. Even though we possess the ability to sell virtually any financial product on the market, we don't receive a bonus for making any recommendations and are paid typically on a fee basis that is completely transparent. As wealth managers, we choose to act in the capacity of independent fiduciary in order to create the highest level of trust possible for our clients. A client going through a divorce is facing an emotionally charged event where there's a great deal of money on the line. Clients gain peace of mind knowing our role and our commitment to helping her with a heightened ethical and legal responsibility.

CHAPTER FIVE

Mediation during a Pending Divorce

As we mentioned earlier, mediation is simply an alternative way to resolve disputes. Approximately 90 percent of all divorces settle in mediation.[6] Mediation is the preferred way to resolve a divorce for several reasons. First, and perhaps most importantly, you have a say in the outcome. If something is agreed upon by you and your husband in mediation, it is binding. In rare circumstances, the judge could step in if something you agreed to is against the state's public policy or the judge feels the agreement is not in the best interests of your children. A judge doesn't always have the time to understand your unique situation. By coming to mediation prepared and ready to negotiate, you have a better chance at getting

---

6   Divorce Statistics, online, http://www.divorcestatistics.info.

what you want and need. We will discuss how to prepare for mediation later in this chapter. A successful mediation proceeding also ends the divorce process and turns off the spigot of professional expenses relating to your divorce.

In mediation, you can also come to an agreement over issues for which the law or the judge could not necessarily address. One of our clients, Haley, had twins reaching college age who both wanted to go to Ivy League schools. Haley wanted her soon-to-be ex-husband, Frank, to pay for all of the children's college expenses. In Florida, parents are only responsible for supporting their minor children until they reach eighteen years of age or they graduate from high school, whichever event comes later (but not beyond age nineteen). After that, they're on their own. But in mediation, Frank agreed to pay for the twins' education as part of the divorce settlement.

Frank is a software entrepreneur. If another software company comes along and successfully competes for Frank's customers, and Frank's income is significantly reduced, he is still legally obligated to pay for the twins' college because he agreed to do so in the mediation agreement. Legally, a judge never would have been able to order Frank to pay the college tuition if the case went to trial. But a judge now has the ability to enforce the agreement.

PICKING THE RIGHT MEDIATOR

Normally, both attorneys will choose and agree on a mediator. We advise working with your attorney to pick a mediator who will allow you to educate them in advance about your divorce and your goals. As such, on the day of your mediation conference, the mediator will already know the facts and issues of your case.

A mediator's advance preparation goes a long way to creating a successful mediation, making the mediation conference more efficient and less costly. Both you and your husband are initially responsible for one half of the mediator's fee (along with your own attorneys' fees for the day). Because mediation conferences could last an entire day or more, you can see the value of working with a mediator who is prepared, making it more likely that your case is settled in the most efficient way possible.

As we have previously discussed, we advise creating charts and/or summaries for the mediator and providing them in advance of the mediation. The mediator will be asked to digest and make sense of a large amount of information in a short period of time. Undoubtedly, they may get confused or make a mistake. Simplifying information for the mediator not only conveys professionalism, but it makes everyone's job easier.

STRUCTURE OF A MEDIATION CONFERENCE

The mediator, a neutral third party, attempts to help you and your husband reach an agreement on various issues and conflicts. Mediators don't make binding decisions; instead, they help both parties assess likely outcomes with the judge. Mediators cannot offer you legal advice.

In Florida, before your case is submitted to a judge for resolution, you are required to attend at least one mediation conference. If the case is settled, the judge will enter a final judgment of dissolution of marriage that incorporates the agreement you and your husband reached at mediation. If there are any unresolved issues, the judge will only know you followed their order and attended mediation to try to resolve the issues. The unresolved issues will be presented to the judge at a trial or hearing for resolution.

If you attend mediation in Florida and do not settle your case, that's okay. The court simply wants to know you both attended the mediation conference in good faith, tried to come to an agreement, but were unable to do so. Mediation is essentially a requirement that must be satisfied before the judge decides your case. Nevertheless, it is best to try to resolve most issues in mediation anyway.

For example, let's say you own a privately held company and have been married for twenty years. You now find yourself getting divorced. Your company possesses valuable intellectual property assets. It is not realistic to expect a judge to be an expert in the complexities of your business. Judges are not business valuators. In court, you may not have the opportunity or sufficient time to provide enough information or context for the judge to understand your unique situation. During a mediation conference, however, you and your husband can make decisions and agreements that would potentially work better for your business partners, your company, and most importantly, your family. Mediation provides you the opportunity to be more creative in crafting an agreement that best suits you and your family's needs.

You don't need to settle 100 percent of your issues in mediation. In Florida, you have the option of going back to mediation as many times as you desire. Partial agreements are common. For example, let's say a couple settles their custody issues and the division of assets in mediation. However, they can't agree on alimony in the first mediation conference. Mr. Smith wants to pay only $4,000 a month; Mrs. Smith wants $7,500. The court is fine with hearing only the alimony issue, and by reducing the issues, you will have significantly minimized the time and cost that the lawyers will spend preparing the case.

THE MEDIATION PROCEDURE

Mediation usually occurs approximately six months after the divorce is filed and three months before a court date. However, the schedule will vary depending on each case. No requirement exists for attorneys to be present at your mediation conference, but it is strongly advised to have representation. The attendees at a mediation conference normally consist of you, your husband, your attorneys, and the mediator. If your husband and his lawyer agree to it, your wealth manager may also attend the mediation conference, offering perspective and helping evaluate settlement proposals. Other experts or forensic valuators may attend as well with the permission of the other party.

During mediation, you and your attorney, as well as your husband and his attorney, are in separate rooms. The mediator travels back and forth between the rooms, negotiating the unresolved issues. It is a confidential process; communications during the mediation conference are not admissible in court and thus cannot be used for litigation purposes. During the process and discussion, you can request that the mediator refrain from sharing specific pieces of information with your husband and his attorney. The average mediation conference lasts up to eight hours but can last longer—sometimes even a couple of days.

A PLAN FOR YOUR MEDIATION

When you are preparing for mediation, you need to evaluate possible settlement outcomes. The first step is to work with your attorney to structure various potential outcomes regarding your goals (i.e., best-case, worst-case, and middle-of-the-road scenarios). Your attorney should then provide these proposed scenarios to your wealth manager who will build different plans based on each scenario. By having an idea of what a settlement will look like, you will be more prepared to estimate what your lifestyle will be post-divorce and on how much money you will need to live. By the time you get to mediation, you should be prepared to know what acceptable settlement offers may be and what they may mean to you in terms of monthly available dollars to pay for all your expenses. It is important that you establish a lifestyle based on your financial means so you do not have to deficit spend; this will inevitably lead to your running out of money.

By having an idea of potential outcomes, you can estimate your monthly cash flow and assess strategic decisions, such as how much it would cost to maintain the marital home if you want to keep it or sell it and downsize. By coming to mediation prepared, you won't be blindsided by the process. You'll have a deep understanding of what any settlement proposal will mean to you.

Our client Gina was married to Brian for twenty-three

years before they decided to divorce. During the marriage, Gina and Brian's lifestyle required expenditures of approximately $32,000 per month. Working with her attorney, we anticipated the following possible outcomes for Gina's upcoming mediation (keep in mind that once divorced, Gina will no longer have the same expenses she did as a couple):

- Possible best-case scenario: Gina receives $3 million in a lump sum payment and $96,000 per year ($8,000 per month) in permanent alimony, resulting in approximately $15,500 per month in funds available.
- Possible middle-of-the-road scenario: Gina receives $3 million in her divorce settlement in lump sum payment and $48,000 per year ($4,000 per month) in permanent alimony, resulting in approximately $11,500 per month in funds available.
- Possible worst-case scenario: Gina receives $2.5 million in a lump sum payment and $27,000 per year ($2,250 per month) in permanent alimony, resulting in approximately $8,500 per month in funds available.

		Monthly Alimony	Total Monthly Cash Flow Available to Gina
Best-Case Scenario	$3 million	$7,500	$8,000/month	$15,500
Middle-of-the-Road Scenario	$3 million	$7,500	$4,000/month	$11,500
Worst-Case Scenario	$2.5 million	$6,250	$2,250/month	$8,500

POSSIBLE MEDIATION OUTCOMES

As we discussed in Chapter 3, the decision to accept or reject a deal is yours, not your lawyer's. Your lawyer is going to work extremely hard to negotiate the best deal they possibly can for you. Because you worked hard to prepare for your mediation conference, you should already know what an acceptable or an unacceptable offer is. However, mediation is a dynamic process. The mediator will share his or her perspective. You are going to have to be prepared to make the ultimate decision, with the help of your lawyer and the rest of the team.

DRAFTING YOUR AGREEMENT

If issues are settled during a mediation conference, an agreement is drafted. The agreement may be a partial agreement if only some of the issues are resolved or a total agreement if all issues are resolved. The mediator (and likely an assistant) drafts a formal document with the negotiated terms and provisions. The process of drafting and revising the agreement may take up to several hours in order to ensure that both parties' intentions and desires are clearly set forth.

Once the formal agreement is completed, the mediator presents it to you, your husband, and both attorneys in separate conference rooms. Everyone reads the document to ensure that it accurately reflects what was agreed to during the mediation conference. The final agreement is signed by you and your husband (along with both attorneys) and becomes binding. The judge will then approve your mediated settlement agreement as a final judgment of dissolution of marriage as if the court decided the case.

On occasion, people experience "buyer's remorse" after the agreement is signed. Or they remember additional items they may want to include in a settlement. Some parties try to change the agreement. This is where a negotiated deal can get shaky.

Occasionally, once the verbal agreement is reduced to writing, the real negotiation begins, even after eight hours of mediation. That's why having an excellent attorney present during the mediation conference is so helpful. They can advise you on whether to sign the agreement, ask for more, or schedule another mediation conference.

Think about the TV reality show *Shark Tank* where entrepreneurs appeal to a panel of venture capitalists to obtain funding for their companies. Sometimes the entrepreneurs ask the "sharks" if they can go out into the hall to discuss the pending offer with each other, a mentor, or a partner. The sharks caution that when the entrepreneurs come back to the room, the proposed terms of the deal may be modified or revoked.

In a mediation, your attorney will help you determine whether or not you could lose the momentum or benefits of a potential agreement by staying late to try to reach an agreement or leaving to try again on another day. They can advise you whether you should accept, reject, or try to change a proposed settlement agreement. In some cases, an agreement cannot be reached even given good faith efforts from both parties. In such a situation, a hearing or trial will be scheduled for your judge to make the final decision(s).

PROS OF MEDIATION

As discussed, mediation provides you a great deal of self-determination during a divorce. You have more of a say in how the marital assets are divided versus allowing a judge to make blanket decisions and superimpose his or her judgment on you and your family.

We are not trying to paint the judiciary in a negative light.

But the truth is that nearly all judges in the United States today have a massive backlog of cases. Hundreds or even thousands of cases may be awaiting a hearing before the judge.

Let's say you go to trial for your divorce, but you aren't scheduled to receive a ruling judge for another month. Between the time your trial ends and the time the judge reviews their notes, they may have had seven or eight other trials, multiple case management conferences, and emergency hearings. If you have a complex divorce, a mediator can spend far more time than a judge working things out.

Not only are judges overwhelmed with cases, but the rules of evidence and court procedures often prevent in-depth testimony that provides a more complete understanding when an issue needs deep consideration. However, such conversations can easily take place during a mediation conference. As previously stated, unlike in a courtroom, everything that is communicated in mediation is confidential. For example, let's say you have evidence your estranged husband is a drug addict and needs help. In a public trial, the danger exists that your husband will be publicly shamed and may lose his job as a result. You do not want that to happen to him, or you and your children will suffer financially. In mediation, the opportunity exists to protect your family's privacy and finances.

DON'T FEAR MEDIATION

Even though the vast majority of all family law cases in the United States are settled in mediation, many people fear the process. The reasons for this fear vary. The mediation conference might be the first time in several months that divorcing spouses have been in the same room together, and the stress of seeing their spouse feels overwhelming—especially if the end of the marriage and the divorce process has been acrimonious. Many people also fear making the wrong decisions in mediation, or they fear the unknown, which is one of the reasons we wrote this book.

The mediation conference can and should be looked at as a way to amicably resolve your pending issues with dignity. Mediation presents the opportunity to put an end to your case and free your life up for your next chapter. Resolution will allow your entire family to move forward, financially and emotionally.

Know where you can push for a better deal and where you cannot. Familiarize yourself with all the issues. Then you will know whether you are receiving a good deal. Mediation is about compromise. It is the rare mediation when one party leaves with an agreement that provides them with 100 percent of what they want. Therefore, it is important to prioritize and focus on the issues that are most important to you.

Mediation is not only about asking for what you want and need but also having realistic expectations. Finally, there is no such thing as overpreparation when it comes to mediation. Remember, this is about the rest of your life, and the vast majority of divorce cases are settled at mediation. Knowing exactly what to expect, what the room looks like, how the conference works, and how long the process might take should provide you with a lot more confidence that this will be the first and hopefully last mediation you will ever have to attend.

It is best to proceed into mediation prepared for a variety of outcomes so that after the process, you will not have buyer's remorse. Instead, you will have confidence that you made the best agreement possible, knowing that nothing is perfect and both parties will have made compromises.

ACTION ITEMS

- Have detailed discussions with your lawyer about how the mediation conference works well in advance of the mediation.
- Determine exactly what you need to provide to your lawyer in advance of the mediation conference to help them help you try to get the best possible outcome.
- With the assistance of your dream team, prepare various possible settlement scenarios so you have a clear plan as to what settlement offers are acceptable and which ones are not.
- Make sure your wealth manager translates what those settlement offers mean to you, in real dollars each month, so you know how much money you have per month following the conclusion of your case.

In our experience of assisting high-net-worth clients after the divorce is complete, we have identified several issues that have routinely caused problems that could have been avoided had we been involved during the divorce process. In the next chapter, we will focus on these "caution flags."

CHAPTER SIX

Caution Flags

In all of our years of assisting clients with wealth management, we have seen the same troublesome issues pop up over and over during and after a divorce. We want to make you aware of (and in some instances reiterate) these cautionary issues so that the same mistakes are not made in your case. These difficulties can be turned into opportunities.

In all high-net-worth cases, attorneys are essential. It is worth repeating: if your husband wants to settle your divorce without an attorney, do not do so. We have repeatedly seen that retaining your own attorney to guide you through the divorce process, gather discovery, and review any settlement proposals should result in a better outcome than representing yourself.

Your husband may pledge to be fair and take care of you. He may suggest going to mediation without attorneys to "just get everything resolved." You may give in to this temptation, but bypassing the normal divorce process could mean very little financial discovery will be produced. For example, if you agree to an equal division of the assets, it is entirely possible you could end up with all the assets with the lowest *cost basis* and the highest capital *gains tax exposure*. This distribution may not result in a truly equitable distribution for you.

Let's look at John and Paula, who live in St. Augustine, Florida. Unbeknownst to Paula, John decided he wanted to get a divorce from her two years ago and began planning how to do so with the least financial impact on him.

At the end of year two, John, a business owner, asked Paula for a divorce and requested that they not use attorneys in order to avoid costs and contention. Paula agreed. John showed Paula a spreadsheet of his company's declining distributions over the past two years. However, if John had shown Paula the corporate tax returns, she would have seen a corresponding increase in retained earnings. The business had increased cash flow in the last two years, but John was diverting it into a corporate "retained earnings" account. Paula did not and would not have known about the increased retained earnings from the documents he provided.

Unfortunately, she agreed to the divorce without attorneys and did not receive her equitable share of the value of John's business. Parties to a divorce case do not have to engage in a protracted and expensive divorce case. But if Paula had hired an attorney and simply received all of the mandatory financial disclosure documents, she could have ended up with a much better outcome.

INVESTMENTS

A settlement may include receiving investment accounts. However, not all assets are created equal, and many people do not take into account what is known as cost basis and the taxes they are required to pay after selling assets. Cost basis refers to the purchase price of an asset and how it is used to determine the capital gains tax you pay when the asset is sold. A capital gain is the difference between the original value of the asset and the price of sale. For example, if you are receiving five hundred shares of Microsoft stock that you and your husband bought twenty years ago, be aware that if you sell it, the capital gains tax will be high because the cost basis is most likely very low.

In sum, when you are analyzing equitable distribution issues, it is not as simple as tallying up the assets and liabilities, putting them on a spreadsheet, and dividing the total by two. If you and your husband have a brokerage account containing $500,000 in cash and an investment account with $500,000 in *stocks*, their after-tax values are not the same. Assume you purchased the stock in the investment account for $100,000 (see the following chart). If you were to sell the stock, you would have $400,000 in capital gains (the market value of the shares of stock less the purchase price of the stock). The tax would result in you writing the IRS a check for $60,000 (assuming you would be paying capital gains tax at 15 percent). So in actuality, the two accounts are an apples-to-oranges comparison. The cash account is worth $500,000, and the investment account is now worth $440,000 after tax. Having a team focused on tax affecting the equitable distribution numbers to ensure you will always be comparing apples to apples could save you significant money in your case.

AFTER-TAX VALUES ARE NOT THE SAME

Cash and Investment Accounts

	Cash	Stock
Value	$500,000	$500,000
Cost Basis (Purchase Price)	$500,000	$100,000
Gain	$0	$400,000
Capital Gains Tax at 15%	$0	$60,000
After-Tax Value	$500,000	$440,000

THE MARITAL HOME AND RENTAL PROPERTY

Cost basis issues also come into play with a marital home. Ray and Kathy bought a house in Jacksonville for

$250,000 and sold it years later for $1 million. A married couple can exclude $500,000 of that capital gain, resulting in capital gains tax on only $250,000 of the gain from the sale. Meanwhile, their neighbor, Jill, bought an identical house with her husband, Leo, at the same time Ray and Kathy did. However, Jill and Leo divorced, and Jill received the marital home as part of the settlement. When, after five years, the upkeep became too much and Jill decided to also sell her home for $1 million, as a single person, she could exclude only $250,000 of the gains and had to pay capital gains tax on $500,000.

Primary Residence

	Married Couple	Single Person
Sold Home for	$1,000,000	$1,000,000
Bought Home for (Cost Basis)	$250,000	$250,000
Exclusion	$500,000	$250,000
Gain	$250,000	$500,000
Capital Gains Tax at 15%	$37,500	$75,000
After-Tax Value	$962,500	$925,000

When it comes to rental property, you must be aware of potential cost basis issues as well. With a rental property, if your CPA has been depreciating the property on your tax returns over the years, it lowers your cost basis, meaning you could pay more in taxes when you eventually sell it. This example illustrates the importance of hiring a qualified team to be on your side during your divorce.

INFLATION AND RISK

Inflation—the increase in the prices of goods and services—is another issue to consider in managing your money post-divorce. A familiar example of inflation is the price of a soft drink. Twenty years ago, you could purchase a Coke out of a vending machine for 50 cents. Today, it is at least $1.25.

When many of our clients first come to us, they are in *capital preservation* mode. Perhaps they haven't worked in two decades, or they grew up poor and fear taking financial risks. They believe that if they just keep their money safe in a traditional bank account, they won't lose anything. Because the value of a dollar decreases over time because of inflation, nothing could be further from the truth!

In the United States, the approximate average rate of inflation over the past twenty years is 2.0 percent a year.[7] Your money needs to be appreciating more than the rate of inflation over time. Otherwise, your money is losing its *purchasing power*. If your alimony payments are fixed, and almost all are, you are going to run into an inflation problem if your investments don't grow over time. At the very least, the return on your investments must exceed inflation.

---

7   "BLS Data Viewer: Report of the Consumer Price Index for All Urban Consumers," BLS Beta Labs, accessed 10/31/20, https://beta.bls.gov/dataViewer/view/timeseries/CUUR0000SA0.

DIVIDING RETIREMENT PLANS
IRAS AND QDROS

An *individual retirement account (IRA)* belongs solely to the person who established it, and you cannot transfer ownership of the IRA or funds between one IRA and another. In the case of divorce, however, as part of equitable distribution of assets, you can do both without penalty or tax consequences. Be advised, however, if you're under fifty-nine-and-a-half years old, you still cannot take the money out of your IRA without incurring a 10 percent early withdrawal penalty (there are some minor exceptions) and being required to pay tax on the amount withdrawn.

However, the IRS has a special rule regarding withdrawal of funds from an IRA following the dissolution of a marriage. If a party to a divorce is due funds from an IRA or 401(k) plan (discussed below), she may withdraw the money directly from the account. She will still have to pay ordinary income tax on this money, but she will not be subject to the additional 10 percent penalty, which would normally apply. We rarely advise our clients to do this unless they absolutely need access to this money.

When it comes to qualified retirement plans such as a 401(k) or 403(b), the federal law requires what is called a *qualified domestic relations order* (QDRO) in order to either divide or transfer these qualified assets, tax- and penalty-free, as part of equitable distribution of the marital estate.

For example, Liz and Richard are getting divorced. Richard has $500,000 in his 401(k) plan, all of it contributed during the marriage. Liz is entitled to $250,000 of the money. The court enters a QDRO and orders the plan administrator of Richard's 401(k) plan to transfer the $250,000 to a 401(k) plan established in Liz's name. This is a nontaxable transfer from Richard's plan to Liz's newly established plan because this transfer was made pursuant to a QDRO.

QDROs are complicated documents, and it's absolutely critical that the drafting and entry by the court of these orders doesn't fall through the cracks. In our experience, it may take several months to get QDROs completed and approved by the retirement plan administrator.

Because it may take several weeks for this money to be transferred pursuant to a QDRO, the amount of money in the account will fluctuate daily until the distribution occurs. As such, there should be language in the QDRO to ensure that each party receives their share of the funds plus or minus the investment gains or losses on his or her share through the date of distribution of the funds. Please make sure you have this language in your final judgment of dissolution of marriage and QDRO. We advise our clients to work with their attorney to ensure completion of the QDROs. A competent attorney should ensure that QDROs are completed correctly.

DEBT AND CREDIT

Knowing how your debts are titled is tremendously important—meaning whose name is on a debt and who is, from the lender's perspective, legally obligated to pay it. For example, on a joint credit card account, both the husband's and wife's name are on the account. If one spouse runs up the credit card bill, it is the legal responsibility (from the creditor's perspective) of both individuals to ensure the debt is covered, even if only one person spent the money.

In negotiating a settlement, you want to make sure you are responsible for any debts in your name. If your husband agrees to pay off any debts in your name and fails to do so, the creditor will still look to you for payment regardless of how your marital settlement agreement assigns responsibility for payment. The creditor does not have the power to look to your husband to pay the debt, as the lender is not a party to your divorce case.

Your credit report lists your credit history and activity, including any debts. You are eligible for a free credit report once per year from each of the three major credit agencies—TransUnion, Equifax, and Experian. Your free credit reports are available at www.annualcreditreport. com.

Before and after your divorce, we recommend you download your credit report, assess if there are any accounts still held jointly with your ex-spouse, and immediately close those accounts. Keep in mind you must have a zero balance to close them. Even though you are no longer married, you are still responsible for paying any debts your ex-spouse incurs on those cards. Meanwhile, if your husband agreed to pay off the credit card debt on a joint account as part of your divorce agreement but forgets or neglects to do so after the divorce, the credit card company will still come after you as the account is still in your name as well. In both these examples, your credit could be adversely affected.

When it comes to the mortgage note on a marital home, it cannot simply be reassigned in your name and your husband's name removed. A mortgage note has to be refinanced, and a lender will not do so unless you qualify. Each lender has its own qualifications. The mortgage rules and regulations constantly change, but at the time of this writing, many lenders require a relatively lengthy history of income from sources such as earnings from employment or alimony. Similar to a credit card company, the mortgage lender cannot be required by the court to remove either party's name from the mortgage note.

ADDITIONAL CAUTION FLAGS

There are four more caution flags of which we want you to be aware. The first is having unreasonable expectations about what you might receive at the conclusion of your divorce case. Although you may be hoping to never have to work again, that may not be realistic. The truth is, you might need to get a job to help support yourself. Doing so may require additional training or earning a degree. And if this is the case, you will need to be prepared to present a specific and reasonable plan in mediation or to the court. It's also important to be aware that in order to secure a loan such as a mortgage or to rent an apartment, you will need a credit and work history of your own.

Second, many couples own rental properties. During a divorce, it is critical that you do your homework to ascertain their true value in order to equitably divide the marital assets. Debt may have accumulated on the properties if, unbeknownst to you, property tax, insurance, and/or condo dues have not been paid.

Third, it is important to retain control over college savings plans and life insurance policies. Your divorce agreement should specify that, no matter who is listed as the account's owner, the funds can only go to the beneficiary. You should also include language prohibiting either party from withdrawing from these accounts without a court order or the agreement of the other party. We had one client whose ex-husband liquidated their child's *529 college savings plan* to buy furniture because he was the "owner" of the plan and their divorce agreement was silent on this issue.

Finally, remember that if your ex-husband is paying you alimony, you will want to have a life insurance policy (or some other form of security) on his life to insure the remaining portion of his alimony obligation. We have seen many women struggle to verify that this life insurance policy is in place long after the conclusion of the divorce case. A great way to make sure you will always have access to information about any such life insurance policy is to have yourself designated as the "owner" of the policy insuring your former husband. Put another way, the life insurance company has no obligation to discuss any policy with you unless you are the owner of that policy—regardless of what your marital settlement agreement provides.

We realize the learning curve may seem steep, so remember not to try to navigate your divorce without a competent team of professionals. With an experienced team, you can successfully encounter every obstacle during and after your divorce, avoiding a lot of the pitfalls we've described in this chapter.

ACTION ITEMS

- You must hire an attorney.
- Understand the after-tax value of all of the assets to make sure you are comparing "apples to apples" when dividing the marital estate.
- Make sure your wealth management team members illustrate how inflation will impact your settlement in the future and how to protect yourself against it.
- QDROs are complicated and are often forgotten. Do not let this happen. Use the post-divorce checklist found in the appendix of this book to discuss the preparation of QDRO(s) with your attorney at the conclusion of your case in order to perfect your interest in your spouse's retirement plans.

One of the most significant assets in a number of high-net-worth divorces is a business that was built (or grew tremendously) during the marriage. Because this topic is so important, we have dedicated the entire next chapter to discussing these issues in detail.

CHAPTER SEVEN

When There's a Business Involved

Divorce can get more complicated when one or both spouses own a business. In these cases, you'll face unique challenges and realities. For example, you may believe that you will obtain half the market value of an extremely successful business when you divorce. Oftentimes, however, that doesn't end up being the case because of laws regarding the division of a business in the context of a divorce. These laws vary from state to state.

Our clients benefit from Caitlin's background as a business valuator. She is able to leverage her previous experience to provide clients with a ballpark assessment of the potential value of the business in question and the relative personal goodwill implications. In situations where there is a disagreement between the husband and wife as to these key components, Caitlin has a strong local network of valuation professionals to whom she can refer clients.

It is essential to hire an excellent business valuator to value the company, preferably one with significant experience valuing businesses in divorce cases. In addition, because judges, mediators, and lawyers don't always possess special expertise or understanding when it comes to analyzing a business valuation report, it is necessary to ensure that your business valuator is skilled in communicating this complex topic to professionals who have little to no familiarity with it.

When Pat was practicing law, he always asked his business valuation experts to prepare a one-page executive summary of the entire report (which sometimes exceeded a hundred pages) explaining the most important information so it could be easily communicated to the mediator and/or the judge (if necessary).

In order to better understand the complexity of a divorce when a business is involved, let's look at the example of Mary and Peter. A decade ago, they started a tech staffing company together. Three years prior to their divorce, they received an offer to sell their company for $20 million. Mary, understandably, believes she co-owns a $20 million business and will receive $10 million in some form or fashion. Mary's expectations may not be correct.

There are two significant components that make up the value of a business. The first is called the *tangible book value*. That is comprised of the value of the office furniture and equipment, the building, its lease, and so forth. The business's debts are subtracted from these assets to arrive at the tangible book value. The second component is called *goodwill*, of which there are two types: *personal* and *enterprise*.

Enterprise goodwill refers to the portion of goodwill that exists regardless of who operates the business. Characteristics that may contribute to enterprise goodwill include location, business model, and business reputation. Personal goodwill is specifically attributable to the owner of the business. Characteristics that may contribute to personal goodwill are personal relationships with customers, technical skills, knowledge, and know-how, and personal reputations. To illustrate the distinction between enterprise and personal goodwill, consider a local insurance agent in your city. Let's say the name of the firm is Jack Jones Insurance Co. Then think of your local State Farm Insurance office with an agent, Rick Smith, managing the office. If you go to Jack Jones's office, it is likely due to personal goodwill because you know, like, and trust Jack. The value of Jack's business is comprised mostly of personal goodwill. If you are one of Rick's customers, it's likely because of the reputation and brand of State Farm and may have little to do with Rick personally. The value of Rick's business is likely comprised mostly of enterprise goodwill.

One of the reasons that Mary and Peter's company has been so successful is because Peter has personally won all the major contracts for their most profitable clients, including the largest hospitals in their city. Peter has a knack for finding the best employees and keeping them happy.

When Peter and his attorney had a business valuation performed on the company, it found $18 million of its value was attributed to Peter's personal goodwill, $1 million to enterprise goodwill, and $1 million to the tangible book value. Even though Mary believed she was going to receive $10 million from the business in the divorce, according to Peter's valuation, she would receive only $1 million: half of the tangible book value and half of the enterprise goodwill. Under Florida law, personal goodwill (the portion of the goodwill attributed to the spouse whose reputation is intertwined with the business) is a nonmarital asset. The following chart illustrates the effect personal goodwill has on the equitable distribution of a marital business in the context of a divorce.

SPLITTING A BUSINESS
The impact of personal goodwill on equitable distribution

		Mary's Half (as per Peter's valuator)
Personal Goodwill	$18,000,000	$0
Enterprise Goodwill	$1,000,000	$500,000
Tangible Book Value	$1,000,000	$500,000
	Total Value of the business: $20,000,000	Total to Mary: $1,000,000

A CASE FOR ENTERPRISE GOODWILL

One of the most important things to remember when you and your spouse own a business is to try to establish that the company possesses more enterprise goodwill than personal goodwill. Remember, personal goodwill is a nonmarital asset in most states.

In Mary's case, she and her attorney disagreed with the percentage Peter's business valuator found to be personal goodwill. Although Peter initially won the big contracts when the business started ten years ago, more recently, Peter hired Bill as his director of business development and sales because Peter was tired of traveling and wanted to slow down a bit. The company had grown substantially since Bill had joined the business. Peter was no longer "the company." The firm had grown, adding more and more layers.

Mary argued Peter was no longer irreplaceable and a new CEO could run the business just as well and maybe even better than Peter. She also argued that customers were now even more attracted to the business due to other employees. Because Mary and her lawyer had such a significant disagreement over valuation, Mary hired her own expert to value the business. Mary's and Peter's valuation experts each agreed the business was worth $20 million. Mary's valuation expert found that the personal goodwill component was worth only $12 million, not the $18 million Peter's expert found. Mary was now in a much better negotiating position.

The couple proceeded to mediation with the two different valuations of the business. After several days of mediation and many arguments about issues such as enterprise versus personal goodwill, the parties reached an agreement. Peter would pay Mary $3.6 million for her share of their business. They both recognized the other's arguments had merit and both saw the risk in their positions if they decided to have a judge make a decision based on the evidence, the valuation reports, and the testimony from the experts.

Of course, Mary still thought she should have received more of a share of the business, and Peter believed he was paying her too much. Still, Mary's decision to listen to her lawyer and hire her own business valuation expert helped her realize $2.6 million more in equitable distribution dollars than she otherwise would have received had she not retained her own business valuator.

It is important to remember that when a settlement is reached, there may not be sufficient *liquid assets* in the marital estate or in the business for one party to buy the other party out of their interest in a business. In Peter and Mary's case, after equitable distribution—dividing up all the couple's other assets, their home, retirement accounts, and so forth—Peter did not have the ability to pay in a lump sum the $3.6 million that he owed Mary for her share of the business. The divorce agreement they negotiated required Peter to pay Mary in monthly installments for her share of the business (over ten years plus interest on the balance) instead of a lump sum.

One of the reasons mediation is so important is that it gives you the opportunity to work out multiple scenarios for achieving a favorable settlement. But it is important to remember that you can't "slay the goose that lays the golden egg." In other words, both parties have to be able to agree to a settlement with which they can comply and not jeopardize the financial integrity of the business.

GET IT RIGHT FROM THE START

A strong team and a thorough plan are essential in a

divorce where a business is involved. You must have an attorney with significant business valuation experience. Further, you must have a top-notch business valuator/appraiser with experience in valuing businesses in the context of a divorce case. Otherwise, you could end up leaving a great deal of money on the table. For example, in Peter and Mary's case, had Mary not hired a competent valuator who produced a technically sound and persuasive report, Peter would have been unlikely to settle at mediation. Under no circumstances would Peter have had to pay Mary $10 million for her interest in the business. If Peter had sensed Mary's lawyer and/or her business valuator were inferior to his, he would have negotiated a better deal or taken the case to trial. Mary's competent business valuator provided the necessary leverage to obtain a better result for her.

As we noted in the last chapter, a spouse who owns a business can also shelter money and/or manipulate income. Kurt owned a security-systems business and started to consider divorcing his wife, Katie, a stay-at-home mom, five years after they were married. For the next three years, Kurt lowered his salary and distributions from his company and socked the cash away in a separate brokerage account of which Katie was unaware. The brokerage account wasn't in Kurt's name but in the name and taxpayer identification number of his business.

When Kurt filed for divorce, Katie had no idea of the additional funds. She was not familiar with the company's books and had never seen the firm's tax returns. Kurt told Katie that his business wasn't worth anything in the present economic climate and that it would be best to leave it out of the divorce agreement. He promised that when he eventually sold it down the line when the economy improved, he would give her half of the sale price. But Katie wasn't going for it. She hired an excellent lawyer and business valuator. By doing this, the business brokerage account and the true value of the company were established, and Katie received what was rightfully hers.

Remember that no matter what your spouse might say, a business can be the most valuable asset in a divorce. If the business is not considered as a part of the equitable distribution of the marital assets, then there's virtually no way to receive your fair share of the marital estate. If the business is considered, then remember that once you finally divide the assets and liabilities, you cannot go back to court and change the terms unless fraud is involved. Get it right from the start and you won't have regrets.

ACTION ITEMS

- A top-notch business valuation expert is an essential member of your team if a business is involved in your divorce case.
- Hire an expert with significant litigation experience and an excellent reputation.
- Learn what information the valuation expert will need from you and provide it to them as soon as possible so they can do their job.

As we mentioned earlier, the supermajority of divorce cases settle. This is not a book about a divorce trial. We are going to assume you are now at the point where a settlement has been reached, and your case has concluded. Congratulations! In the next chapter, we will focus on moving your wealth management team from a supporting role to a directing role, and you will learn how we help our clients begin to make the transformation to their new life.

CHAPTER EIGHT

Merging Wealth Management with Your Divorce Case

As you near the end of your divorce case (if you have taken our advice from the previous chapters), you should be ready to implement your wealth management plan. Having several million dollars' worth of investment accounts, retirement accounts, real estate, and/or some debt transferred to you with a financial strategy in place, you should feel confident your wealth management plan is already established and ready to be activated.

Every investment firm is different and has its own way of doing business. In this chapter, we explain our process and what we believe to be best practices. Our process begins simultaneously with your divorce case. Having an understanding of your goals is necessary for us to build a wealth management plan that will help you accomplish those goals, while providing you with the peace of mind and confidence you deserve.

Living in Florida, we are exposed to hurricane season annually from June to November. The local news, The Weather Channel, and other sources track the "cone" of the hurricane, meaning the projected path of the storm. Reports cannot specifically predict how the hurricane will affect you and your home. A meteorologist won't say, "Jeanne, you live at 346 Main Street—the storm surge is going to flood your house at 3:00 p.m. Evacuate now and don't plan on being able to return for two months." Or, "Jeanne, this storm isn't going to affect you other than you will be without power for two days."

Although we can go years without suffering a direct hit or even a near miss, everyone living in Florida knows that a hurricane plan is a necessity. The same is true for your divorce. However, unlike The Weather Channel, which can only provide information, we provide direction and advice to our clients and their lawyers to create a wealth management plan based on a range of specific outcomes likely to occur in their divorce cases.

We dig much deeper than The Weather Channel forecast by providing you with a detailed plan, with several different scenarios. We sincerely hope a wealth manager is part of your divorce team to provide a range of specific outcomes for you. Our job is to make sure you understand the possible results. Furthermore, it's our job to work with your attorney and the other experts on your team to increase the likelihood that your desired outcome will be your more likely outcome. We create a wealth management plan to reassure you in the same way a hurricane strategy does—by having storm shutters, a generator, food and water, an evacuation route, alternative housing, and cell phone service.

Now we are going to discuss our philosophy and our unique wealth management process, which explains all of the components we feel should be included by a comprehensive wealth management plan. Perhaps you have worked with a financial advisor or a wealth management professional in the past and realize your advisor did (or did not) advise you on all of the variables of wealth management described below. From our experience, we know all of these variables are important, and the best financial outcomes usually occur when they are all considered together.

Our wealth management process is best described by the following process.

INVESTMENT MANAGEMENT

Investment Management (IM) is the process of managing the growth of your assets over time, and generating the income necessary to support your lifestyle. Depending on how much money you need for fixed and variable costs, we determine what average rate of return is required to help you accomplish your goals.

Your average required rate of return will determine which types of investments will be included in your investment portfolio. For example, how much should be invested for growth and how much should be invested for income? To get a better understanding of these important pieces, let's define a few key terms related to the types of investments you might have in your investment portfolio.

STOCKS

Stocks can also be referred to as equities. A stock is defined as a partial ownership share of a company. When you own a stock, you do not get to call the CEO and tell him or her what to do. However, you are able to vote on certain issues to help set the general direction of the company. As the company grows, expands, and performs well financially over time, the price/value of the stock normally increases. In addition, most companies will pay their shareholders a portion of profits in the form of dividends. Dividends are income and cash flow to the investor.

The price of all companies' stock fluctuates based on the value investors assign to the company. For example, our client Monique owned an insurance company with her husband, Chip. Their agency originally sold property and automobile insurance, but it grew into a successful business and expanded the types of insurance products it offered to their customers.

When Chip filed for divorce, they had been in business for twenty years, and the company's revenue had increased from $50,000 per year to over $4 million per year. As a private company, the value of the company stock had grown substantially over time. (How much it is worth could be decided by a business valuation, discussed in Chapter 7, or by selling the business.) If Chip and Monique decide to sell the firm as part of their divorce settlement, another insurance company would make an offer based, in part, on the perceived value of future profits, and the sale would involve purchasing the private "stock" of the company. In sum, the value of the stock, whether it is the stock of a small company such as Chip and Monique's insurance agency or the stock of a public company such as Microsoft or Apple, can increase or decrease in value based on market conditions and many other factors.

The other component of stock is the cash flow distributed to shareholders. In the case of Chip and Monique, they would pay themselves and their employees a salary, pay all of their business expenses, and whatever remained was profit. Sometimes a company will retain some of its profits for future development (such as buying another company, upgrading equipment, or purchasing a new building). The remaining cash is sent to shareholders as dividends. This is true with both private and public companies. Over time, as the company and its profits grow, the dividend should also increase. This can be the other benefit of owning stock—receiving increasing dividends, which means potentially more income to you, the investor.

BONDS

Bonds, also referred to as fixed income, are a promise to repay a debt. A good analogy is a mortgage. When you buy a home, you put cash down (a down payment) and then you obtain a loan from a bank to pay the remaining purchase price. Let's say you purchase a $500,000 home with a down payment of 20 percent or $100,000, leaving you with a mortgage of $400,000. The loan (commonly referred to as "the mortgage") has a term (thirty years) and an interest rate (4 percent). A bond is similar to a mortgage. With a bond, you are the mortgage holder and the bond makes interest payments to you.

As a way to finance operations and raise money to expand their facilities or purchase new equipment, many companies use bond financing. So does the US government, which issues bonds to the public in the form of Treasury Bills (less than one year in maturity), Treasury Notes (one to ten years in maturity), and Treasury Bonds (ten to thirty years in maturity). Investors buy these bonds, and our government promises to pay interest during the period stated on the bond (maturity) and return the principal (the original price you paid for the bond) to the investor at the end of the term.

Bonds are an important part of an investment portfolio because they provide both stability to the portfolio (generally fluctuating less than stocks) and a steady income stream. As we assist our clients in creating a wealth management plan, income from stocks and bonds are extremely important parts of their portfolios.

ASSET ALLOCATION

Asset allocation indicates the way a portfolio is constructed to accomplish your goals. Professional wealth managers have decades of data on both risk (fluctuation) and return on investments (growth and income) as they relate to how equity and fixed-income investments should be combined in a portfolio.

Think of baking a cake. To do so, you need specific amounts of flour, eggs, baking soda, baking powder, a little oil, sugar, and vanilla. How you combine those ingredients determines whether you end up with a cake or a soufflé. It is the same with an investment portfolio—a portfolio comprised of mostly bonds or fixed income will result in lower returns but also lower fluctuation (lower risk), while a portfolio comprised mainly of equities or stocks should result in greater returns over time but with much higher fluctuation (higher risk).

The key in deciding the right recipe for our clients is what rate of return they need in order to accomplish their goals. This type of investment process to build a portfolio designed by our clients' goals is called *goal-based investing*. We measure our clients' investment performance by the success relative to their personal and lifestyle goals. Our focus and approach shift from trying to "beat the market" (which is extremely difficult and risky to do) to achieving our clients' personal goals. This process helps us make sure our clients choose investment strategies in order to achieve life goals—such as paying for college for their children or grandchildren, funding weddings, and/or retiring at a specific age. In the next chapter, we will discuss how we measure progress relative to a client's wealth management plan when we describe our Financial Progress Report™.

A word on risk, or fluctuation: everyone we work with dislikes it when his or her portfolio declines in value, but fluctuation means a portfolio both increases and decreases in value. For all clients, there are two types of risks we worry about. The first is market risk, the risk of losing your money. In a well-diversified portfolio of stocks and bonds, this can be reduced. Most of the portfolios we construct for our clients contain holdings in thousands of different stocks and bonds through mutual funds and *exchange-traded funds* (ETFs).

The second risk, however, is even more dangerous. It is a risk of inflation or the loss of purchasing power. As a reminder, inflation occurs when the costs of goods and services increase over time. Your income must increase as well to purchase the goods and services you need and want.

Think back to the price of your first car or home. If you bought your first new car in 1973, it likely cost around $3,000. Today, that same car type would cost around $30,000. That's an example of inflation. If you earned a salary of $6,000 per year in 1973, you likely would have been able to afford a new car, depending on your other expenses and your ability to finance the purchase of the car. If your annual salary is still $6,000 per year today, it is highly unlikely you would be able to purchase a new car.

Because of inflation, salaries generally increase so as to afford the ability to purchase goods and services. If you have thirty years or more of life expectancy in front of you and you rely on your portfolio for income, the loss of purchasing power is your biggest risk—not the fluctuation in the value of your portfolio's assets.

There are several ways to go about owning stocks or bonds. First, you can research and purchase individual stocks and bonds. We do not recommend this type of investment strategy because it is difficult to get *diversification*. It is even more difficult to fully know and understand a company's financial situation. It is also difficult to know when to buy and sell.

Second, you can purchase a *mutual fund*, which is a collection of stocks or bonds managed by a professional money management team. Historically, this has been the most popular way for individual investors to own a diversified portfolio. When you own a mutual fund, you own a piece of the fund. The fund manager owns the portfolio of stocks (which vary by fund type and objective and can range from a small number of securities into the thousands). The fund is priced at the end of the trading day.

With a mutual fund, you generally get diversification and professional money management. Such management comes with a cost (the manager and the fund family charge a fee for the research and management of their fund). These fees can range from near zero to well over 2 percent of your assets in the fund per year.

The third way to own stocks and bonds is through an ETF. ETFs generally have lower expense ratios than actively traded mutual funds. In addition, an ETF is priced throughout the day like a stock. An ETF owns a select group of stocks or bonds. Many ETFs track an index such as the Dow Jones Industrial Average (consisting of thirty of the largest and most well-known US companies) or the Standard and Poor's 500 (made up of five hundred of the largest companies in the United States). ETFs tend to be more tax efficient than mutual funds because they do not have to distribute their capital gains every year like most mutual funds do. We tend to favor ETFs in nonretirement accounts and save mutual funds for retirement accounts. Because retirement accounts grow tax-deferred, capital gains distributions are not a concern.

LIFE MAP

In the asset allocation section above, we described the importance of understanding our clients' goals, because their goals dictate how we build their portfolios. We ascertain our clients' goals through what we call our Life Map process, which we first discussed in the introduction of this book. A client's Life Map is developed after we ask the client a series of questions focused on seven primary areas:

- Values most important to them
- Life goals
- Family and significant personal relationships
- Interests and hobbies
- Assets
- Preferred involvement in the wealth management process
- Existing professional advisors

This extensive interview provides a 360-degree understanding of who our clients are and what they are trying to accomplish for themselves and their families. The Life Map is shared with every member of your wealth management team. The personalized analysis puts your entire team on the same page with his or her role in executing your wealth management plan. An example of a Life Map is in the appendix at the end of this book.

For our clients going through the divorce process, once

we know what assets and support (alimony and/or child support) they are likely to receive, we can then determine how much investment return their portfolio must generate in order to accomplish their goals. If, for example, a client's portfolio needs to achieve only a 4-percent rate of return on average over time to accomplish his or her goals, then we will construct his or her portfolio with primarily fixed income (bonds) and little growth (stocks).

However, most of our clients need a rate of return on investments greater than 4 percent. Generally, the greater the required return, the greater percentage of equities we will need to include in our clients' portfolio relative to fixed income to help them accomplish their goals.

Diversification acts to reduce *market risk* in a portfolio by including equities and fixed-income investments; large-cap (large companies), mid-cap (medium-sized companies), and small-cap (small companies) equities, including domestic and international; investment-grade bonds; high-yield bonds; and cash. This approach of maximizing returns and minimizing risk is called modern portfolio theory (US economist Harry Markowitz is considered the father of modern portfolio theory and won a Nobel Prize for his work in 1990). The goal is to sufficiently diversify a client's portfolio to minimize risk. Once we have created each client's unique portfolio, it will need to be rebalanced as markets fluctuate. Market fluctuation will eventually make our clients' balanced portfolios unbalanced. For example, if the large-cap portion of a portfolio is supposed to be 30 percent of the portfolio and is now 20 percent as a result of market fluctuation, this portfolio needs to be rebalanced by selling a portion of other assets that are overweight and buying those for the portfolio that are underweight.

HYPOTHETICAL ASSET ALLOCATION/ REBALANCING GOAL

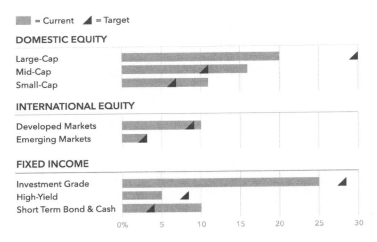

Consistent *rebalancing* must be part of any sound wealth management plan. To illustrate the importance of rebalancing a portfolio, consider the following example. During the COVID crash between February and April of 2020, we called our client Elizabeth, who was in a panic. She had been watching CNBC all day. "You've got to sell everything in my portfolio immediately," she told us. We told

Elizabeth to stand up, walk over to the television, and turn it off. We reminded her that our philosophy is to be proactive, not reactive. We already had a plan in place for what was happening, and her portfolio would be rebalanced.

When the stock market decreases, stocks go on sale. In a broadly diversified portfolio, that may be the time to buy. When the market increases, that is the time to trim stocks at a profit and buy bonds. As Warren Buffett puts it, "Be greedy when others are fearful and fearful when others are greedy."

Finally, part of our investment management process is to ensure that we work in tandem with our clients' CPAs and always be mindful of reducing tax exposure as it relates to their investments. We always want to be aware of the tax consequences of a transaction before we complete it. Because federal income tax laws change annually, new tax saving strategies are required.

ADVANCED PLANNING

For many financial advisors, their planning for you ends at the Investment Management stage. But advanced planning (AP) is a critical part of what we do and what we believe is essential when it comes to any successful wealth management plan. Our advanced planning process focuses on the following four areas:

- Wealth Enhancement (WE)—Includes strategies we can implement to help our clients increase their cash flow, decrease taxes, and decrease debt when applicable.
- Wealth Protection (WP)—Involves making sure our clients have all of the necessary and cost-efficient insurance products to protect their assets in case of unforeseen circumstances.
- Wealth Transfer (WT)—Plans for the most tax efficient and easiest way to transfer our clients' wealth to their beneficiaries.
- Charitable Giving (CG)—For our clients who are charitably inclined, this stage focuses on implementing a charitable giving process to ensure funds go to our clients' desired charities with the least amount of tax exposure.

WEALTH ENHANCEMENT

Wealth Enhancement involves many factors and includes having a deep understanding of our clients' tax situations. In the midst of a divorce, the tax return provides not only important information about how our clients functioned financially when married but also provides clues as to how to plan for their new future as single taxpayers.

Think of the tax return as a treasure hunt. When analyzing our clients' tax returns, we often find forgotten or hidden assets that generate interest and dividends, as well as information concerning the sale of a business/real estate. The tax return also helps your team plan for your receipt of an equitable distribution of the marital estate from your divorce case. Further, the tax return helps us evaluate if assets should be invested to generate tax-free income for those in higher tax brackets. In Wealth Enhancement, we, in concert with our client's CPA and attorney, use strategies to increase cash flow, decrease or eliminate any potential debt that will be outstanding after the divorce is final, and minimize taxes.

Let's look at some additional aspects of Wealth Enhancement.

Pensions/Qualified Retirement Plans

An excellent wealth management plan ensures that any pensions or retirement plans you receive in your divorce are properly allocated to you. To do so, the court enters an order typically called a qualified domestic relations order (QDRO) after the conclusion of your case in order to divide and/or transfer retirement assets, tax- and penalty-free, as part of the equitable distribution of the marital estate. It is essential that all of the requirements necessary for a QDRO are completed so you receive the benefits to which you are entitled. Your lawyer will help you with this process. However, as we discussed in Chapter 6, QDROs are often neglected, and as a result, the nonparticipant (nonemployee) spouse's entitlement is not apportioned to him or her by the plan's administrator.

Social Security

If you have worked more than forty "quarters" of employment—meaning a three-month calendar quarter—you will likely be eligible for your own Social Security benefit. You may also be eligible to claim a portion of your husband's Social Security benefit. The Social Security rules can be confusing. As you build your wealth plan, it is important to include how and when to take your Social Security benefit.

In general, for every year that you wait to receive your own benefit after you reach full retirement age as determined by federal law, your benefit increases by 8 percent (guaranteed by the government) as well as any inflation (cost-of-living) increase. This continues until age seventy. For a spousal benefit, the increase generally stops at your full retirement age (as defined by Social Security law), which for most people is somewhere between the ages of sixty-six and sixty-seven. If you were married for ten years or more, you could receive benefits under your ex-husband's reward (even if he is remarried).

WEALTH PROTECTION

Wealth Protection concerns protecting that which you currently have, as well as assets and future income you will receive in your divorce. This includes the proper titling of your assets (homes, businesses, cars), ensuring you have the proper types of insurance (automobile; liability, including an *umbrella insurance policy*; flood and/ or excess flood and property insurance; long-term care insurance; disability insurance; and life insurance). If you are going to be receiving alimony, life insurance may be required on the life of your former husband to secure his alimony obligation.

For the insurance, your former husband would usually be required to pay the premiums, and if he dies, you will receive a lump sum amount of money to compensate for the alimony he can no longer provide. It is critical you own the policy. If your ex-husband owns it and decides to stop paying the premiums, the policy will lapse, and you will probably never know, even if you were designated as the beneficiary. Life insurance can also be used to fund college, pay off a mortgage or other debt, provide legacy assets for your children and grandchildren, or provide for your favorite charity.

You will need to have what we call emergency savings (cash). These are funds that are easily available for emergencies and to afford you peace of mind. Everyone has his or her own idea of how much money should be part of their emergency fund, and this needs to be incorporated into your wealth management plan. This amount is usually equal to three to six months of your monthly living expenses.

Health Insurance

We always advise our clients that they cannot afford to be without health insurance at any point in time. It is a critical aspect of protecting your wealth. If you have been receiving insurance through your husband's plan or employer, you may be eligible for continued health coverage post-divorce for thirty-six months, under what is called COBRA (which stands for the Consolidated Omnibus Budget Reconciliation Act, a law passed by Congress in 1985).

If you cannot continue as a dependent on his plan, you will have to purchase health insurance on your own. This can be confusing and costly, but again, that is why a wealth management team is so important. Your wealth management plan must include determining the cost of health insurance both before and after Medicare, the federal insurance program that provides health insurance for most people at age sixty-five. Medicare, however, does not cover all healthcare expenses, so supplemental health insurance is necessary. We work with our clients to make sure they apply for Medicare at the appropriate time and help them obtain the additional insurance they need.

WEALTH TRANSFER

Wealth Transfer involves having the proper estate planning documents so that if you become incapacitated or pass away, the wealth you have created is used for your care and reaches your beneficiaries in the way you intended. Documents such as a power of attorney, a healthcare power of attorney, a will, a living will, and trusts must be redrafted post-divorce. Meanwhile, if you ever decide to remarry, a prenuptial agreement should be thoughtfully considered and integrated into your estate plan. Like tax laws, estate planning laws change annually. We stay abreast of the significant changes in these laws and regularly advise our clients to revisit their estate plans with their attorneys when their circumstances and/ or changes in the law require it.

CHARITABLE GIVING

Charitable giving is especially important to most clients once they exceed their wealth management goal. Once that happens, many clients like to know how much they can give on an annual basis to charity. Sometimes setting up a *donor-advised fund*, an instrument specifically designed for philanthropy, or a family foundation will make sense. Such a structure will allow you to benefit those organizations important to you, while at the same time potentially reducing any estate tax due at your death or your tax liability during any given year.

RELATIONSHIP MANAGEMENT

Relationship management (RM) is all about ensuring that our clients receive the communication, tools, and service they need to understand their wealth management plan and be able to work with their team when questions or concerns arise. RM has two parts: (1) client management and (2) expert management.

CLIENT MANAGEMENT

Client management (CM) involves discovering the most efficient way to communicate with our clients. Do they like to be contacted via phone, text message, or email? Do they want to receive paper copies of their account statements, access to their statements online only, or a combination of both? How often would they like to review their plan, and do they prefer to do that in person or via an online meeting, Zoom, or another platform?

EXPERT MANAGEMENT

You may already have your team in place, or as we mentioned in Chapter 1, you may need to find all new team members, which ideally should consist of a CPA, an estate planning attorney, and a wealth manager. Whether it is the old team, a new one, or some combination of the two, your wealth manager should use Expert Management (EM) to ensure that every member of your team (1) is involved in your plan, (2) understands what you want and need, and (3) knows how you want to communicate. The wealth manager should serve as the "quarterback" for your team.

ANGELA'S STORY—A COMPREHENSIVE CASE STUDY

Let's look at the aspects of how the Wealth Management Formula works through the eyes of Angela. Angela is fifty-two years old and received approximately $6 million in her divorce settlement—$3 million is in an IRA, $2 million in an investment account, and $1 million in equity in her house. Angela isn't receiving alimony or child support, and she doesn't have a mortgage or any other debt. After taking her through the Life Map exercise we previously described, we determined she needed $20,000 a month to maintain her lifestyle, requiring a 7 percent rate of return from her investment portfolio for the remainder of her life.

When Angela started her divorce, she did not have her own relationships with any financial professionals: no CPA, no estate planning attorney, no property or casualty insurance agent, and so forth. Her former husband had historically created and maintained all of those relationships. As part of Relationship Management (RM), we recommended that Angela consult with all those professionals. She interviewed candidates over the phone. When Angela picked the professionals she liked best, we set up appointments and accompanied her to the initial meetings with each one.

Under Investment Management (IM), an investment account was designed for Angela placing 60 percent in a diversified stock portfolio for growth and 40 percent in bond funds for income. For her IRA, we also used a similar 60/40 allocation but chose mutual funds because traditional IRAs are not taxed until money is withdrawn—so we did not have to be as concerned with capital gains distributions in her IRA.

On the first of the month, $20,000 was automatically sent from Angela's investment account to her bank account. This stream of income is akin to Angela receiving a monthly paycheck. In addition, she created an emergency savings account at the bank with $120,000 from her divorce settlement, which she keeps in a money market at her bank. When Angela unexpectedly needed a new air conditioner, she was able to withdraw $5,000 from this emergency account to pay for it. Financially, Angela did not skip a beat.

In the arena of Wealth Enhancement, because Angela is fifty-two years old, no portion of the $20,000 she receives per month currently comes from her IRA; instead, it comes from her investment account. In most cases, Angela cannot withdraw money from her IRA penalty-free until she is fifty-nine-and-a-half years old—early withdrawal would result in a 10 percent penalty from the IRS, in addition to being taxed as ordinary income.

Meanwhile, Angela drives a BMW and has a tendency to drive a little fast. If she causes an accident, the other driver could sue her. If Angela were found to be liable, her $2 million investment account would be exposed or unprotected. Under Wealth Protection, she secured an umbrella insurance policy protecting all of her investments in a worst-case scenario.

Her team advised Angela to sign the appropriate

documents to remove her name from the title of her twenty-five-year-old daughter's car. The reason: if her daughter rear-ends someone and that driver sues, Angela would be liable as well and could potentially lose the funds in her investment account because she was listed on the title to the vehicle as one of the owners of the car.

Angela also purchased long-term care insurance. Such insurance protects Angela's assets should she become unable to perform the activities of daily living and ensures her daughter will not have to serve as her primary caretaker. Long-term care insurance was much less expensive for Angela to buy now rather than later, given her relatively young age.

Under the Wealth Transfer part of the formula, arrangements were made for Angela's IRA to transfer, in the event of her death, to her beneficiary, her daughter. Her home and investment account were put into what's called a revocable living trust. Creating the trust ensures her assets will pass on to her daughter without going through probate proceedings—an often-lengthy and expensive legal process of proving the validity of a will.

As far as the charitable giving component of the formula, Angela has a generous spirit and wanted to continue to contribute to nonprofits as she did during her marriage. Her husband worked for Johnson and Johnson (JNJ) for twenty years, and $100,000 of the $2 million in her investment account was JNJ stock. Because the stock was purchased so long ago, if Angela sold it in order to donate the proceeds to the causes she loves, she would have to pay substantial capital gains tax. Instead, we helped her open a donor-advised fund, a financial instrument specifically designed for philanthropy. The JNJ stock was placed in the fund, and now Angela can gift the stock to any qualified charity without having to pay the capital gains tax she otherwise would have had to pay if she sold the stock to donate cash to charity.

As you can see, Angela's financial situation is unique and relatively complicated. There are a lot of variables that needed to be considered in order to provide her with a comprehensive wealth management plan. She has implemented her plan and is thriving because she now has the confidence she did not have at the initial stages of her divorce. Angela has a reasonably clear idea of what her financial future looks like. She knows the limitations of what her wealth management plan will allow her to do.

We hope you will see a lot of parallels between your situation and Angela's. We hope you will work with a wealth manager during your divorce to help your lawyer identify all potential financial issues in order to plan for them. If you do so, you will be able to hit the ground running at the conclusion of your case.

In the beginning of this chapter, we discussed the importance of a wealth management plan to ensure that you attain safety and peace of mind in very much the same way a hurricane plan helps Florida residents prepare to safely respond to a dangerous storm. Angela's plan gave her a rock-solid sense of financial stability for her post-divorce future. With a strong team and a solid wealth management plan, you can have the same.

ACTION ITEMS

- Make sure a wealth manager is an integral part of your divorce team in order to prepare for the multitude of financial issues you will need to deal with before, during, and after divorce.
- Preferably work with a wealth manager who has substantial experience working with divorce-related issues.
- Be thorough in discussing your goals with your wealth management team so your team can construct a portfolio that will be best suited to help you accomplish your goals.
- Keep your wealth advisor updated immediately whenever there are any changes to your financial circumstances or goals.
- Consider hiring a divorce advocate to help you through the divorce while simultaneously helping you prepare for your financial future post-divorce.

In the next chapter, we'll take a look at what things should look like in your future from a wealth management perspective. We'll discuss what you should expect from your wealth management team going forward and how the team keeps you on plan so you can live the life you want to live.

CHAPTER NINE

Your New, Exciting Future

We hope you've come to the conclusion that it is truly possible for you to move beyond the final judgment of your divorce to long-term financial security. We have seen countless clients do so. As wealth managers and the authors of this book, our passion and commitment to helping people successfully navigate divorce and become financially secure is rooted in our own backgrounds.

While practicing family law in Florida, Pat saw the need for people to have support when going through the complex and often contentious and emotionally draining process of divorce. As an experienced business valuator as well as having earned CFA® and CPA credentials, Caitlin brings a level of professional knowledge that is hard to match. We believe the combination of our expertise, coupled with our laser-focused dedication to our clients, is what has created so many successful outcomes. We're "all in" with all of our clients.

Nobody marries thinking they will get divorced. If you are like many of our clients, you are an intelligent, trusting individual whose husband may have managed the marital finances for the last two or three decades. Or you may have been the higher-earning spouse during the marriage who was in control of the finances and have to pay a lot of your hard-earned savings to your ex-husband. Perhaps your situation falls somewhere in between. No matter what, a divorce creates a breakdown in trust and a sense of bewilderment about how to go forward in a financially astute way. You are in the process of rebuilding your life and need access to the best information possible.

Whomever you hire as a wealth manager, look for not only an excellent and reputable firm but also one that has a partner on board with a legal background. By doing so, issues in a divorce will likely be identified early so mistakes can be avoided.

REGULAR MEETINGS

After your divorce, it is paramount that you continue to meet regularly with your wealth management team. Your advisors should conduct periodic review meetings where you discuss issues, such as changing life circumstances and the need to increase cash flow and/or decrease taxes (and avoid tax mistakes).

Your financial progress should be monitored, especially when it comes to Social Security, retirement, and estate planning. Your insurance needs (life, disability, long-term care, and so forth) must be reviewed, and your team needs to assist you in living within your means and adjusting to unexpected events such as illness or paying for your son or daughter's wedding. Life and the economy are always changing, and your financial plan must change with it.

It is common to feel fear about being in charge of your finances, perhaps for the first time in your life. Your team should help you overcome common fears, such as running out of money, losing your assets in some sort of embezzlement scheme, getting seriously ill and becoming a burden to your kids, and/or not having enough money to leave as a legacy. We want to assure you that confidence will come with knowledge and time.

ANNUAL FINANCIAL GOAL

We believe it is vital to have an annual financial goal. We create one for every client, for every year of his or her life, and then subsequently monitor it with our Financial Progress Report™. A sample can be seen in the Financial Progress Report™ graphic. At review meetings, we are able to easily determine whether our client is on or off track relative to his or her goal.

Coming in ahead of the goal means a client can give more to his or her children, to his or her favorite charities, or to him- or herself. Coming in behind plan calls for analysis: the client may be spending too much, or the financial markets may have shifted and the portfolio needs rebalancing. Tough decisions may be in order, such as delaying big purchases and travel or not being able to purchase a new car. The annual financial goal is the most efficient way to gain this perspective. It also gives a client confidence and reduces anxiety.

Two years after our client Daphne's divorce, we met with her for a review meeting. Daphne's year-end goal number was $5.8 million, and her portfolio had grown to $6 million. With the $200,000 excess amount ahead of her goal, Daphne was able to take her three adult children on a family vacation to Australia and New Zealand—a bucket-list trip for her! She also gifted to charity $50,000 via some of her exchange-traded funds (ETFs) which had a low cost basis through a donor-advised fund. By using this tax-reducing strategy, she did not have to pay capital gains tax on the charitable gift.

FINANCIAL PROGRESS REPORT™
Client: Daphne, June 2020

Tax-Deferred Accounts	IRA 6GY***000	$1,500,000
Tax-Free Withdrawal Accounts	ROTH IRA 6GY***001	$200,000
Total of Tax-Deferred Accounts		**$1,700,000**
Taxable Accounts	Investment 7J4***000	$4,300,000
Total Taxable Accounts		**$4,300,000**
TOTAL VALUE OF ACCOUNTS		**$6,000,000**

Goal of Ending Assets in December 2020 is $5,800,000 for $180,000 of annual after-tax cash flow. *Daphne is $200,000 ahead of plan, which she can keep investing to stay ahead of plan or use for vacations and/or charitable giving.*

REVIEW OF ADVANCED PLANNING

We discussed advanced planning earlier in the book (for the full discussion, see Chapter 8), but we want to touch on key points one more time. First, it is imperative that you arrange to obtain your own health insurance. Again, two options exist: (1) if you are on your husband's policy from his employer, you can continue to receive it for three years after the divorce through a program called COBRA (but you will pay the full cost of the premiums unless a different arrangement is negotiated in your mediated settlement agreement), or (2) purchase your own plan. After your case ends, if you are not working or receiving coverage from an employer, you must find an insurer on your own in order to ensure there is no lapse in your health insurance coverage.

Next, beneficiary designations must be updated on your life insurance policies, IRAs, and retirement plans, especially on employer-sponsored plans such as a 401(k) plan if you are working. All insurance policies must be updated to ensure that you are the policyholder. Your home must be properly insured.

In Florida, flood insurance is important. You also need automotive and homeowners or renters insurance in the proper amount, as well as an umbrella insurance policy to minimize your financial exposure if someone is severely injured on your property and you are sued as a result of the injury.

Finally, your trust (if applicable) and will must be updated. In Florida, an estate attorney will typically prepare two additional documents along with your will. The first is a designation of healthcare surrogate, which designates who will make healthcare decisions for you if you're incapacitated or unable to make these decisions on your own. The second is a power of attorney, which assigns the financial decision-making authority to another person or persons if you are unable to make the decisions.

NEW RELATIONSHIPS

It is entirely possible that you will meet a significant other and want to move in or start a new life together. Remember, a new relationship has financial implications. For example, Florida has a law where alimony can be modified or reduced if the recipient spouse enters into what is called a financially supportive relationship.

Bottom line: if you move in with someone (or vice versa), you are potentially jeopardizing part of or all of your alimony award. Don't commence this type of relationship until you discuss the implications with your lawyer.

If you decide to get remarried, we strongly suggest you visit your lawyer and consider the possibility of a prenuptial agreement at least eight weeks before the date of your wedding. It is far too easy in a new marriage to comingle your finances and thus convert what was once a separate or nonmarital asset into a marital asset. If you want your children to inherit your money, provisions as to what happens in the event of your death while you are married to your new spouse must also be included in your prenuptial agreement.

Conclusion

This book is based on thousands of experiences with our clients. With each one, our combined knowledge base has grown and our ability to serve our clients has strengthened. When you hire a wealth management team, they know that every divorce is unique. There's no one-size-fits-all approach to your divorce. You must have a team that can navigate the circumstances of your particular situation, with all its complexity, and advise you accordingly.

To maximize your chances for success in your divorce and afterward, let's review the four tenets we discussed in Chapter 1:

1. Assemble a team of competent advisors who regularly communicate with you and with each other.
2. Have a written plan.

3. Keep the process as simple as possible.
4. Be an optimist; everything is going to work out.

One of the most challenging emotions for most of us is uncertainty. Having a wealth management team that can evaluate your best-case and worst-case scenarios helps you feel prepared and confident. You are better able to expect what might happen during and after your divorce.

In Chapter 1, we discussed our client Jan, whose divorce was dragging on for months. With overwhelming bills each month from her attorney, the stress was crushing her. When we first met her, Jan had extreme anxiety and was having difficulty eating and sleeping. With her children off at college, she was alone for the first time in her life. With time, patience, and counseling, Jan eventually became a strong and independent woman, fully capable of taking care of herself emotionally and financially.

Divorce can often seem to strip a person of his or her identity and sense of belonging. Jan navigated that terrain and emerged from her divorce financially educated, confident, and excited about her future. She has returned to her volunteer work with the Humane Society and recently threw a benefit for the nonprofit that was well attended and featured in the local newspaper. She now feels like a valued member of her community again, and her lifestyle is more complete and financially secure than ever. Jan is like the vast majority of our clients who are living amazing, financially secure, and abundant lives post-divorce.

That's the best reward we could have expected. We know the same kind of peace and independence awaits you. We hope you use this book as a guide. Step by step, you can find your way to a new life.

If you have any questions about this book or what we do, we would love to hear from you. Email us at info@ullmannwealthpartners.com.

Appendix

LIFE MAP

Sample Client

Values
- Freedom
- Security most important
- Be self-sufficient

Goals
- Stay in current home
- Maintain lifestyle
- Don't run out of money
- Perform more community service
- Live off $180,000/year (gross)
- Relax
- Live by water
- Two big trips per year
- Get youngest daughter through college

Relationships
- Pets
  - Ernie (6yo Labrador Retriever)
- Children
  - John (age 24)
  - Amanda (age 18)
- Julia, best friend, Naples
- Mother, lives in Orlando
- Jane, college roommate

Interests
- Travel
- Animals (Humane Society)
- Tennis
- Yoga
- Literacy

Assets
- Primary residence
  - $800,000 value, $300,000 mortgage at a 4% interest rate
- $6 million in investment and retirement accounts

Process
- Communication
  - doesn't check personal email often
  - face-to-face/phone call preferred
  - doesn't like texting
- Micro manager
  - tends to be anxious
  - doesn't want to give up all responsibility
  - needs control and to understand finances
- Results = less anxiety

Advisors
- No CPA
  - Spouse did taxes
- Attorney
  - Family law
  - Estate Planner
- No life insurance agent
- No wealth manager
- Spouse took care of all finances

A STANDING FAMILY-COURT ORDER

IN THE CIRCUIT COURT FOURTH
JUDICIAL CIRCUIT IN AND FOR _____
COUNTY, FLORIDA

CASE NO:
DIVISION:

In Re: The Marriage of

,   Petitioner,

and

,   Respondent.

STANDING FAMILY LAW COURT ORDER[1]

The following Standing Court Order shall apply to both parties in an original action for dissolution of marriage, separate maintenance, or annulment. The Order shall be effective with regard to the petitioner upon filing of the petition and with regard to the respondent upon service of the summons and petition or upon waiver and acceptance of service. The following Order shall remain in place during the pendency of the action, unless modified, terminated, or amended by further order of the Court upon motion of either of the parties:

1. Neither party shall sell, transfer, encumber, conceal, assign, remove or in any way dispose of, without the consent of the other party in writing, or without an order of the court, any property, individually or jointly held by parties, except in the usual course of business or for customary and usual household expenses or for reasonable attorney's fees in connection with this action.

2. Neither party shall incur any unreasonable debts, including but not limited to, further borrowing against any credit line secured by the family residence, further encumbrancing any assets, or unreasonably using credit cards or cash advances against credit or bank cards.

---

1   First Amended Order, effective for all petitions filed on or after April 1, 2016. Original Order entered on or about April 1, 2003.

3. Neither party shall permanently remove the minor child or children of the parties from the State of Florida, without written consent of the other party or an Order of the Court.

4. Neither party shall cause the other party of the children of the marriage to be removed from any medical, hospital, health, and/or dental insurance coverage, and each party shall maintain the existing medical, hospital, health, and dental insurance coverage in full force and effect.

5. Neither party shall change the beneficiaries of any existing life insurance policies, and each party shall maintain the existing life insurance, automobile insurance, homeowners or renters insurance policies in full force and effect.

6. If the parties have a child or children in common, a party vacating the family residence shall notify the other party or the other party's attorney, in writing, within forty-eight hours of such move, of an address where the relocated party can receive communication. This provision shall not apply if there is a conflicting Court Order.

7. If the parties seek to relocate more than fifty (50) miles from their present residence and have at least one minor child in common, the relocating party shall comply with the requirements as set forth in Florida Statute Section 61.13001.

8. If the parents of the children live apart during the dissolution proceedings, they shall assist their children in having contact with both parties, which is consistent with the habits of the family, personally, by telephone, audiovisual communications, and in writing unless there is a conflicting Court Order. All parties shall within ten (10) days update his or her mailing address with the Clerk of Court any time his or her mailing address changes.

9. Pursuant to the administrative orders issued in the Fourth Judicial Circuit (Duval, Clay, and Nassau Counties) and pursuant to Section 61.21, Florida Statutes, parties to a dissolution of marriage action with minor children shall complete a four-hour parenting course, such as

the Putting Children First in Divorce Course offered by Hope Haven (http://www.hope-haven.org/divorce-counseling) or a similar qualifiedin-person program within forty-five (45) days after the date of filing the petition in the case of the Petitioner, or within forty-five (45) days from the date of service of the petition in the case of the Respondent. Parties shall file the Certificate of Completion in the Court file promptly.

10. If the parties have at least one minor child in common, the parties are notified that Florida Statute Section 61.13(2)(c)(1) provides that: "It is the public policy of this state that each minor child has frequent and continuing contact with both parents after the parents separate or the marriage of the parties is dissolved and to encourage parents to share the rights and responsibilities, and joys, of childrearing. There is no presumption for or against the father or mother of the child or for or against any specific time-sharing schedule when creating or modifying the parenting plan of the child."

DONE AND ORDERED in chambers, in _Duval_ County, Florida, this _9th_ day of _March_, 2016.

_____
Administrative Judge

Cc: Petitioner _____   Respondent _____

Failure to obey these orders may be punishable by contempt of court. If you wish to modify these orders, you must file an appropriate motion with the Family court Clerk's Office in the county where the action is pending.

Service of standing Order shall be made with service of process of a petition for dissolution of marriage, separate maintenance or annulment.

YOUR POST-DIVORCE CHECKLIST

ADMINISTRATIVE

- ☐ Settle all outstanding bills with your legal counsel and other divorce professionals.
- ☐ Review your final judgment/marital settlement agreement carefully.
- ☐ Name change: If applicable, change your name.
  - ☐ Social Security Administration: Complete the application for a Social Security card (SSA Form SS-5), then mail it and supporting documents (or take them to your local Social Security Office). This service is free.
  - ☐ Driver's license: Appear at any driver's license office with proof of your legal name change and a certified copy of your divorce decree. There is a charge for this service.
  - ☐ Change name on passport and other documents.
  - ☐ Notify all of your creditors, banks, employer, and so forth of the change.
- ☐ If you move, notify all applicable parties of your address change.
  - ☐ Forward your mail. Complete the official change of address form online at usps.com or at your local Post Office.

COPARENTING

- [ ] Pay all support when due as required by the divorce decree. Keep detailed records of the same.
- [ ] If you change jobs, notify your new employer of any court-ordered support, if required by the income deduction order to do so, to effectuate continued automatic withholding.
- [ ] Keep your scheduled visitation times with your children.
- [ ] If applicable, execute IRS Form 8332 to transfer dependency exemptions to the other parent as set forth in the divorce decree.
- [ ] Consider using an application such as Our Family Wizard (ourfamilywizard.com) to help facilitate coparenting and information sharing between parents, if necessary.

DIVISION OF ASSETS

- [ ] Divide all personal property as set forth in the divorce decree.

REAL PROPERTY

- ☐ Execute and/or make sure that your former spouse executes any and all quit-claim deeds to transfer title to real property as required by the divorce decree.
- ☐ Remove your former spouse's name from your lease/ mortgage via refinancing, if necessary.
- ☐ Complete the process of refinancing or assumption of mortgages.

CAR TITLES

- ☐ Transfer the title(s) to your motor vehicles to reflect the ownership as set forth in the divorce decree. (Tip: Complete a Notice of Sale [HSMV Form 82050] and mail to the Department of Highway Safety and Motor Vehicles to avoid any civil liability for the operation of said vehicle. This form can be found at www.flhsmv.gov.)
- ☐ Notify your auto insurer of any changes in drivers, ownership, and addresses.

QUALIFIED DOMESTIC RELATIONS ORDER (QDRO)

- ☐ If applicable, ensure that the QDRO is entered and implemented as required by the divorce decree.
- ☐ If applicable, change the beneficiaries on all retirement and pension accounts as set forth in the divorce decree.

ESTATE PLANNING

- ☐ Execute a new will/trust.
- ☐ Designate guardians for your children, if necessary.
- ☐ Update your healthcare proxy and power of attorney documents.
- ☐ Contact us for a referral to a qualified estate-planning attorney.

FINANCIAL ACCOUNTS AND CREDIT

- ☐ Make sure your name has been removed from any debts/loans that are no longer your responsibility. (Tip: Please note that agreements between the parties are not binding on third-party creditors, and in the event of a default payment, creditors have the right to seek recovery from any party that was originally responsible on the debt.)
- ☐ Close all joint accounts (banking, brokerage, etc.), and open new accounts in your name only.
- ☐ Close all joint credit accounts. (Tip: Obtain a credit report thirty days later to verify no joint accounts remain. You can obtain a free report at annualcreditreport.com.)
- ☐ Establish credit in your name.

INSURANCE

□ Change the beneficiaries on your plans and policies (e.g., life insurance, deferred compensation), if permissible under the divorce decree.

□ If applicable, obtain life insurance naming your former spouse and/or children as beneficiaries to ensure continued support if you should die, as set forth in the divorce decree.

□ If applicable, ask for proof from your former spouse that they have obtained the required insurance.

□ Revise health insurance coverage for your former spouse and/or dependents as set forth in the divorce decree.

□ Execute all necessary COBRA documents to ensure continued health insurance coverage, or make sure that your former spouse has done the same.

Glossary

403(b) Plan: A US tax-advantaged retirement savings plan available to certain employees of public schools, some nonprofit employees, cooperative hospital service organizations, and self-employed ministers in the United States.

529 College Savings Plan: A tax-advantaged method of saving for the future education expenses of a designated beneficiary.

Answer to the Petition for the Dissolution of Marriage: Formal response to the Petition of Dissolution of Marriage.

Asset allocation: Distributing investment funds among categories of assets, such as cash equivalents, stock, fixed income, and many others. Asset allocation affects both risk and return and is a central concept in financial planning and investment management.

Bonds: Any interest-bearing or discounted government or corporate security that obligates the issuer to pay the bondholder a specified sum of money, usually at specific intervals, and to repay the principal amount of the loan at maturity.

Capital gains tax: A type of tax levied on profits an investor realizes when she sells a capital asset for a price that is higher than the purchase price.

Capital preservation: An investment strategy where the primary goal is to preserve capital and prevent loss in a portfolio.

Cost basis: The purchase price of an asset and how it is used to determine the taxes (capital gains) paid when the asset is sold.

Deposition: A witness's out-of-court testimony, in writing (usually done by a court reporter), to be used in court or for the purposes of discovery.

Discovery: The relevant information each party collects in order to settle or litigate a case.

Diversification: The process of allocating capital in a way that reduces the exposure to any one particular asset or risk. A common path toward diversification is to reduce risk or volatility by investing in a variety of assets.

Donor-advised fund: A financial instrument specifically designed for philanthropy. It allows donors to make a charitable contribution, receive an immediate tax deduction, and then recommend grants from the fund to any IRS-qualified public charity over time.

Enterprise goodwill: One of two types of goodwill, which is a component used in determining the value of a business. Enterprise goodwill refers to the portion of goodwill that exists regardless of who runs it, such as the business product, model, and location.

Equitable distribution: The process of dividing the assets and liabilities in a divorce.

Equity: See *stocks*.

Exchange-traded fund (ETF): A security that tracks a particular set or combination of equities, bonds, or an index but trades like a stock on an exchange.

Expert witness: A professional who has a certain expertise that will help the court understand a certain issue or help arrive at a value of an asset.

Fiduciary: A person or legal entity that has the power of responsibility of acting for another in situations requiring good faith and total trust.

Final judgment: The document that ends the divorce case and sets out each party's rights, responsibilities, obligations, and entitlements.

Financial affidavit: A sworn statement of each person's sources of monthly income and expenses, all assets and the estimated value of those assets, and any liabilities and the current balance of each one. This document is arguably the most important document in the entire divorce case.

Goal-based investing: A type of investing that aims to attain specific life goals (e.g., kids' college education or retirement) instead of measuring market returns.

Individual retirement account (IRA): An investing tool that allows an individual to save for retirement on a tax-advantaged basis.

Liquid assets: A resource that can easily be converted into cash and used to pay for goods and services or pay off liabilities.

Mandatory disclosure documents: Sixteen financial items that both parties are automatically required to produce within forty-five days of when the original divorce petition was filed.

Market risk: The possibility of an investor experiencing losses due to factors that affect the overall performance of the financial markets.

Mediation: A confidential proceeding used by a couple to attempt to settle all or part of the issues related to divorce.

Mediator: A neutral third party whose goal is to try and help you and your husband reach a settlement of the issues in your divorce.

Mutual fund: A fund operated by an investment company that pools money from shareholders and invests in a portfolio of stocks, bonds, or other securities.

Personal goodwill: One of two types of goodwill, which is a component used in determining the value of a business. Personal goodwill refers to the portion belonging to a specific individual running a business, such as their reputation and personal skills.

Petition: A formal written request, appealing to authority with respect to a particular cause.

Petitioner: The spouse who initiates the process of divorce by filing the petition for dissolution of marriage.

Purchasing power: The value of a currency in terms of the goods or services that one unit of it can buy.

Qualified domestic relations order (QDRO): A court order for a retirement plan to pay child support, alimony, or marital property rights to a spouse, former spouse, child, or other dependent of the plan participant.

Rate of return: The gain or loss on an investment over a specified time period, expressed as a percentage of the investment's value.

Rebalancing: The action/trading strategy of bringing a portfolio that has deviated from one's target asset allocation back to the target.

Respondent: The spouse who is legally served the petition for dissolution of marriage filed by the petitioner.

Schedule K-1: A tax document that reports each shareholder or partner's share of income, losses, deductions, and credits.

Shared parental responsibility: A court-ordered relationship where both parents continue to enjoy full parental rights and are required to make joint decisions regarding the health, welfare, and education of the children.

Stocks: Ownership of a corporation represented by shares that are a claim on the corporation's earnings and assets.

Tangible book value: A component used to determine the value of a business. For example, this may refer to the office furniture and equipment, the building, its lease, and so forth.

Timesharing: The amount of court-ordered time each parent will spend with the children.

Trustee: An individual who holds and administers property or assets for a beneficiary.

Umbrella insurance policy: Extra liability insurance coverage that goes beyond the limits of the insured's home, auto, or watercraft insurance.

About the Authors

PATRICK J. KILBANE J.D., CDFA®

Pat joined Ullmann Wealth Partners to assist, guide, and support individuals before, during, and after they begin the dissolution of marriage process. Before joining the firm, Pat concentrated his law practice in matrimonial and family law. For nearly a decade, he represented high-net-worth individuals in their divorce cases. Pat was a shareholder at a prominent 300-plus-attorney statewide law firm in Florida.

Pat is extremely active in the Jacksonville community and serves on numerous boards in the area. He has received two gubernatorial appointments—one as a Board Member to the Jacksonville Aviation Authority and the other one to the 4th Circuit Judicial Nominating Committee. Pat served as chairman of both of these boards. In 2020, Pat was elected to the Adrian College Board of Trustees.

Pat earned his JD from the University of Notre Dame and a BBA from Adrian College, from which he graduated summa cum laude. He is also a Certified Divorce Financial Analyst®.

CAITLIN FREDERICK, CFA, CPA

Caitlin is the Director of Financial Planning and a Wealth Advisor. Her primary role is to lead and enhance the financial planning process for all of our clients, but especially likes working with the clients who utilize our Divorce Advisory Services.

Prior to joining Ullmann Wealth Partners, Caitlin worked in the Valuation and Capital Markets groups at PwC for over five years. Most recently, Caitlin worked for a local boutique investment banking firm performing business valuations.

Caitlin earned a Masters in Accounting and Valuation and a BA in economics from Vanderbilt University. She is a member of the AICPA and the CFA® Society of Jacksonville.

Caitlin and her husband have two young daughters and live in Atlantic Beach. She is active in Rotary International and the Association for Corporate Growth. In her spare time, she enjoys practicing yoga and going to the beach with her family.

Made in the USA
Columbia, SC
06 May 2021